What Schools Can Be

What Schools Can Be

A Guide for Educators

Rick Ackerly

ROWMAN & LITTLEFIELD
Lanham • Boulder • New York • London

Published by Rowman & Littlefield
An imprint of The Rowman & Littlefield Publishing Group, Inc.
4501 Forbes Boulevard, Suite 200, Lanham, Maryland 20706
www.rowman.com

86-90 Paul Street, London EC2A 4NE

Copyright © 2024 by Rick Ackerly

All rights reserved. No part of this book may be reproduced in any form or by any electronic or mechanical means, including information storage and retrieval systems, without written permission from the publisher, except by a reviewer who may quote passages in a review.

British Library Cataloguing in Publication Information Available

Library of Congress Cataloging-in-Publication Data

Names: Ackerly, Rick, author.
Title: What Schools Can Be: A Guide for Educators / Rick Ackerly.
Description: Lanham, Maryland: Rowman & Littlefield, [2023] | Includes bibliographical references. | Summary: "In entertaining stories of teachers, children, parents and principals Ackerly shows leadership in action and defines the elements of educational cultures, how culture is the delivery system for education, and how individuals can be leaders and create the culture of whatever group they are in"—Provided by publisher.
Identifiers: LCCN 2023030887 (print) | LCCN 2023030888 (ebook) | ISBN 9781475873467 (cloth : acid-free paper) | ISBN 9781475873474 (paperback : acid-free paper) | ISBN 9781475873481 (ebook)
Subjects: LCSH: Educational anthropology—United States.
Classification: LCC LB45 .A324 2023 (print) | LCC LB45 (ebook) | DDC 306.430973—dc23/eng/20230808
LC record available at https://lccn.loc.gov/2023030887
LC ebook record available at https://lccn.loc.gov/2023030888

♾️™ The paper used in this publication meets the minimum requirements of American National Standard for Information Sciences—Permanence of Paper for Printed Library Materials, ANSI/NISO Z39.48-1992.

To

My Children:

Brooke, Peter, Lizzie, Katie

My Grandchildren:

Annlyn, Aasha, Elijah, Dana, Anna, Abdallah, Musa, Ilyas, Zoe

Contents

Foreword		ix
What Schools Can Be: A Guide for Educators		xi
Acknowledgments		xv
Introduction		1
1	Don't Get Mad; Get Creative	5
2	Thank You for Criticizing	7
3	Arrogance Is a Learning Disability	11
4	In Education, Failure Is an Option: New Myths for Successful Kids and Better Schools	15
5	Measure What Matters	21
6	The Culture We Create Is Visible in Everything We Do	27
7	First-Grade Teacher Designs a Learning Organization	33
8	A Leadership Culture Is Obvious to All	37
9	Real Authority Brings out the Authority in Others	41
10	Don't Teach Empathy. Teach Thoughtfulness	45
11	A Culture with the Soul of Creativity	53
12	Conflict Aversion Is a Learning Disability	59
13	Conflict Is the Crucible of Character	65

14	Conflict Is Required for Creating Character	67
15	Treat Kids As If Social Responsibility Is a Natural Act	73
16	To Get Results, Schools Must Be in the Friendship Business	81
17	Home Schooling Is an Oxymoron	85
18	The "Soft," "Non-cognitive Skills" are Hard, Cognitive, and Learned in Community	89
19	Social Deprivation Causes Cognitive Deprivation	93
20	Perfectionism Is Another Disability	99
21	Staying out of Trouble Is Not a Worthy Mission	103
22	The Need to Contribute Is a Childish Impulse	109
23	Building an Organization on the Need to Contribute	115
24	Diversity: The Solution, Not the Problem	117
25	Authority that Brings out the Authority in Others	127
26	Teacher Authority, Boundaries, and the Business of School	131
27	Authority, Imperfection, and Behavior Problems	137
28	True Authority Leaves Room for Others to Exercise Their Authority	139
29	Integrity: Bringing Your Whole Self to the Table	147
30	In Times of Crisis the Nomenclature Must Be Changed	155

Appendix: Counter-Cultural Habits, Mores and Myths	167
Essential Skills in Learning Organizations	167
Mores of Learning Communities	169
New Myths for Educational Cultures	170
Notes	171
Author Biography	173

Foreword

I have admired Rick Ackerly's work in education and insights about child development for many years. A longtime school principal, he understands the kind of leadership that creates educational communities where kids learn to thrive. He also knows how to tell a beautiful story that captures imaginations and recognizes diverse experiences.

This collection of chapters reflects Rick at his best—knowledgeable, a keen observer of human behavior, candid, and creative. Filled with great moments of clarity, learning, and love, Rick shows us how relationships are key to leading a meaningful life of purpose and well-being. Rick's true respect and love of children permeate the pages of this book. Creating winners and losers doesn't help kids grow to their full potential. Building exceptional relationships based in love is the key to every child's success. Period. As Rick shows us, love is hard but necessary work. It involves deep learning, creativity, collaboration, and resilience.

I suggest you sit back and enjoy the stories in this book. They just might transform the way you see American education and how good it can be when parents, schools, children, and communities learn together through respectful and loving relationships.

Marilyn Price-Mitchell, PhD
Author, *Tomorrow's Change Makers: Reclaiming the Power of Citizenship for a New Generation*
Founder, RootsOfAction.com

What Schools Can Be
A Guide for Educators

Preface

Failure of the American school system to educate has been known for over a century. It was Mark Twain, after all, who famously said, "I never let my schooling interfere with my education." But more than a century of school reform has shown that this is easier noticed than accomplished.

Why? Because the delivery system for education is not the curriculum or the standards or the textbooks or the testing. The delivery system for education is culture, and the American public school system was designed early in the industrial revolution to sort rather than to educate. It was designed to sort for who should be the leaders and who should be the workers.

Wave after wave of "reform" has not changed the culture of schools. Schools fail not because of low standards or curriculum or poverty or parents or privatization or technology or textbooks or money. They certainly don't fail for want of trying. They fail because of culture.

Culture is the delivery system for education because, whatever the curriculum is, children's brains are constructing their own content from the context in which the curriculum is delivered. They are minute-by-minute making a mental map of how the world works and how they can make it work. School culture shapes their brains. The context determines what they make of the content. If democracy is taught in an authoritarian culture, the kids are not learning democracy. They are learning how to function in an authoritarian culture.

There are, of course, schools that do deliver an education, and this book gives us examples. I have been working in, leading, and visiting schools since I was three years old. There are two kinds of schools: leadership communities and achievement mills. The former educate and the latter merely sort. The former empower people to be ahead of the change curve in an increasingly complex world. The latter? Well, they inspire lines like: "When I think back on all the crap I learned in high school, it's a wonder I can think at all" (Paul Simon, 1973).

I was lucky enough to attend schools that delivered education, and went into the profession knowing that school *can* be an education. At the age of twenty-nine, I got an opportunity to be the principal of a school in Kansas City. The school was in such bad shape that I was the only one they could find to take the job, and they thought I would only last a year.

I fooled them. I not only lasted eight years in the job, but more importantly, after three years, the school was thriving. Soon it was the hot school in Kansas City with long waiting lists. That was the beginning of my career as an architect of school culture.

To borrow from Leo Tolstoy: all effective schools are alike; each dysfunctional school is dysfunctional in its own way. Twenty minutes in a school is all you need to know whether you are in a leadership community or an achievement mill. You can feel it. Words like enthusiasm, joy, and love pop into the brain. You see creativity in the academic work gracing the walls. You see kids collaborating on schoolwork in the classrooms. Everyone seems to love learning (surprise, surprise).

What are the design elements of an educational culture? What can you do to make sure you get an education and help other people get one, too? *What Schools Can Be* answers these questions. This series of snapshots show the design elements of a culture that actually delivers education and prepares young people not only for work but also for leading, loving, and thriving in a rapidly changing world.

Whether you are a parent concerned about your children or a teacher who is called to educate, whether you are an administrator or a board member accountable for the education of some young people, whether you are a citizen or bureaucrat or politician concerned about the future of our nation, whether you are a child or adolescent concerned about humanity or the future of the planet, or simply a person trying to get an education, this book is for you.

In July of 2011, there was a "Save our Schools March" in Washington. "Take back our schools!" was the war cry, but in all the speeches there was no "I have a dream" speech: what it would look like if teachers and parents were to "take back the schools?" What would it look like if the schools were actually led by educators? This book answers those questions.

These stories focus on children. Why? Because if you spend any time with children and you don't come away with a better understanding of what a school should be, you haven't been paying attention to the right stuff. Watching children in action reveal the many facets of creative, leadership cultures and the kind of leadership required to build and maintain them.

My hopes are three: to change mindsets about the elements of culture required for optimal learning, to increase the tools in our toolbox for creating such cultures, and to increase our understanding of children. You may even get a few ideas about how to lead your life the way you most want to lead it.

Acknowledgments

It's high time to acknowledge some of the great educators who are in these stories although some of their names have been changed. Elizabeth McClellan, Anola Picket, Suzanne Abbey, Debbie Meyer, Victoria Podesta, Gretchen Ott, Beth Campbell, Marianne Dunlap, Mary Anderson, Laroilyn Davis, Barbara DeMoss, Terry Ashkinos, Candy Mabry, Deirdre Fennessy, Margaret Piskitel, Martha Ochoa, Ben Petrofsky, John Hooker, Dan Schwartz, Alicia Perdue, Anne Ryan, Ray Burns, Michael Kuhn, Mike Margolis, Judy Stone, Matt Ronfeldt, Susan Porter, Kirk Bell, Brittany Musler, Peter Doyle, Andre Perry, Diane Fiorella Carroll, Kathy Winkler, Peggy Swenson Fowler, Edie Quinby, Karen Beraldo Ginsberg, Jaime Vallar, Fern Stampleman, Ellen Baru, Randy Bowman, Dorothy Marks, Cheryl Lexton, Rebecca Kroll, Sarah Elizabeth Ippel, Kit Land, Dan Larson, Josh Stern, Joan Fitzpatrick, Ginny Spivey, Madora Soutter, Kalindi Handler, Peter Bokor, Kirk Koenigsbauer, Nicola Valentino, Mary Fasenmyer Robinson, Nicole Bessalo, and Tracy Kirkham, Tina Corse, and many other great educators whose wonderful work is reflected in this book. You made my career and gave me the material for this book.

Credit for the cover photo goes to Dennis Gray and John Kraus. The three students on the cover: Enzo Klaus, Margo Mitchel and Zander Levenburg are now in college.

I also want to thank some of the people who had a hand in helping me shape this book: Allan Stern, Larry Arnstein, Patricia Lathrop, David Watts, Betsy, Chuck and Henry Cordes, Mark Lauden Crosley, Jon Madian, John Berman, Donna Volpitta, John Hendrickson, Tracy Kirkham, Sally Mahe, Marty Dutcher, Susan Porter, Paul Chapman, Jim Ackerly, my daughter Elizabeth Ackerly, and my wife Victoria Podesta.

Introduction

Do you realize that it is distinctly possible for a child to reach the age of 18 without ever having done something upon someone else depends?

—Urie Bronfenbrenner speaking to educators and parents in 1975

Recently, the mother of a fourth grader told me of the struggle her daughter, Ashley, had with social anxiety.

In first grade, for instance, she would freeze when it was her turn to speak to the class. The very thought of doing a book report in front of her classmates would cause her to shake. Sometimes she would be so terrified that the teacher would have her sit outside the circle or in her own corner of the classroom.

It was a topic at parent-teacher conferences, of course, for several years. Often teachers would suggest diagnoses like "social anxiety disorder" and suggest plans for helping her, like not looking at her classmates when she spoke in class or inviting small groups of best friends to her home. Various kinds of behavior modification were suggested and tried, but nothing worked. In fact, it seemed to get worse. If she were required to speak in front of her class, she froze in terror.

The mother wanted to diagnose the problem and come up with a plan to fix it. Her husband and her husband's family all thought the appropriate adult response was not to make a big deal about it and just wait for it go away, as in "She will grow out of it." The situation caused a rift between the mother and her in-laws, and of course, exacerbated marital challenges.

Then, in fourth grade, Ashley wrote a great story. Her teacher praised her for a great piece of work and showed it to her former first-grade teacher.

They decided that the first-grade teacher should ask Ashley if she would like to read it to the first graders.

She did, and Ashley agreed—flattered to have been asked. As the day of her presentation approached, Ashley showed no signs of her normal anxiety. On the day of her presentation, she walked proudly into the room like an actress, sat in the speaker's chair with twenty-five first-graders at her feet and read her story with great articulation and even flare.

She was so successful at this that Ashley's teacher arranged for other speaking engagements and Ashley even performed at an all-school assembly—with no signs of stage fright or even nervousness. Yet, Ashley still panics before making a presentation to her class.

It is, unfortunately, standard procedure for parents and teachers to try to diagnose a "problem," and then prescribe. Listening to adults talk about students who are experiencing challenges you would think, there are only a handful of diseases: dyslexia, ADHD, sensory motor integration, social anxiety disorder, autism spectrum, and a few others.

Adults have a hard time seeing school from the child's point of view and rarely ask. When parents and teachers talk about children, they often forget five obvious and critical truths about humans:

1. our uniqueness,
2. our nearly infinite complexity,
3. that we are not the same person today that we were yesterday,
4. that we know things about our own problems, and
5. that our brains are always working the problem in their own invisible way.

To say that Ashley has "social anxiety disorder" is about as helpful a diagnosis as telling a person who is shivering and too weak to get out of bed that he has "fever." The medical model doesn't work when it comes to education—in fact it is usually counter-productive. Naming a problem usually begs the question of what to do about it, only some of the prescriptions work with some of people some of the time.

All of us humans are at risk for three major diseases: loneliness, boredom, and uselessness. And the cures are simple: collaborate, create, and contribute.

In the end, what worked for Ashley was that her teachers noticed the unique details of Ashley's experience in school and thought creatively about it. Ashley's difficulty speaking in groups is her own unique version of a challenge we all have: how to be your imperfect self and avoid embarrassment at the same time. Ashley addressed her social anxiety by *working with* her teachers to *create* something of *value* to her classmates.

Education is a profession laced with problems. In an educational institution, problems are understood to be opportunities for learning, for education, for growth. In schools that educate, problem is not a dirty word, and there are no problem kids.

"Problem" is not the only word we need to use differently. Throughout these stories you will notice different understandings for some very common words. My physics professor at Williams College, Robert Parks like to say: "In times of crisis the nomenclature must be changed." That was true in physics a hundred years ago (when they coined the word "quantum"), and it is true in education, now.

Getting this nomenclature right is important because the language that we use and the meanings we attach to them drive our thinking and our thinking drives our actions, and these actions reveal the school culture.

Here are some of the key words: leadership, authority, discipline, creativity, intelligence, disabilities, "non-cognitive skills," challenge, diversity, social responsibility, character, genius, and what it means to "be a good student." We need to understand how criticism, conflict, diversity, mistakes, and failure are good things. My definitions are summarized in chapter 30.

Right off the bat, we need a more functional definition of the word education. Education stems from the Latin *educare*, to lead out. *Education is leading our unique character out into the world to contribute creatively and collaboratively to it.* Education is leadership. Education is leading brains out, not stuffing information into brains.

The core concept embedded in this new glossary of terms is that a leader's job is to define her character in such a way as to increase the authority of others, thus creating relationships in which all people define their unique characters in partnership with their genius. These concepts are central to a loving, learning, leadership culture.

What Schools Can Be shows people of all ages, all backgrounds, and all positions in society doing just that—sometimes in surprising ways, sometimes in ways that are so common we don't even notice and take them for granted, missing our own educational opportunities—the opportunity to change our minds.

So, what should a school be? A school should be a place where adults and children love to go every day to work together creating cool things and making a difference.

CHAPTER 1

Don't Get Mad; Get Creative

Genius, n 1. The tutelary spirit of a person, place or institution.

—Oxford English Dictionary

Letting go of control and letting go of "self" long enough to change our mindset are important habits for leading our lives and the lives of others. Paradoxically, this is what is required for us to be free to define self creatively to each new situation.

Elizabeth had a classic class clown in her second-grade class one year. Ruben was smart, active, inquisitive, and made the class laugh several times a day, disrupting Elizabeth's lessons. She found him infuriating, but fury was not recognized as an acceptable professional approach. By the third week of the year, she was sending him into the hallway for a "timeout" as a regular practice. That Friday, she lost her temper and sent Ruben to the principal's office.

Over the weekend Elizabeth worried, thought, wondered, pondered, stewed, and talked to a friend about what she should do to fix this problem. Only three weeks of school! It just couldn't go on like this. Nonetheless, Monday morning she arrived at school without a plan.

Luckily, Ruben was the first student into the classroom that morning. She stopped her class preparations and gave him her usual big smile that accompanied her usual friendly, "Good morning, Ruben."

A happy "Good morning," was Ruben's reply.

"Did you have a nice weekend?"

"Yes, Ms. Prior"

"What did you do?"

"I watched 'Princess Bride.'"

"Did you like it?"

"It was hilarious! I loved it."

"I know. I love that movie. I have watched it a hundred times."

Then, Elizabeth was struck with inspiration. "You are a comedian, aren't you?"

"YES!" He said with his biggest grin ever and even a little embarrassment.

"I know. I see that in you." And just then another student came in. Elizabeth greeted him and then went back to preparing for class.

As if by magic, Elizabeth was suddenly free from her anxiety about Ruben. She had an idea. She lay in wait for Ruben as she and the class went through her planned activities. Her moment came sooner than expected.

As one student was leading the calendar-based math activity, another one piped up: "The red ones are all odd numbers."

Ruben jumped in with "That's odd." Everybody laughed, including Elizabeth. "That's funny," she said. "You made a pun."

The lesson continued, and Elizabeth kept her ears open.

A few minutes later, Ruben responded to another student's observation with a sarcastic remark. The student slumped.

"That's not funny," said Elizabeth. Ruben's face fell. He participated constructively with no more jokes until recess. In his reading group after recess Ruben made another joke and Elizabeth laughed, "That's another good one."

For the rest of the day Elizabeth pointed out good jokes and simply said: "That's not funny" to ones that were distracting, hurtful, or disruptive. Before long Ruben was working with her instead of against her, and Elizabeth had her best teaching year yet.

Elizabeth's creative leadership was an important piece in making her classroom an educational institution.

We all want our children to be self-confident learners who are good at working with others and comfortable in their own skin. We want them to be authorities who exercise that authority in ways that increase the authority of others, leaders whose leadership brings out leadership in others. And of course, children naturally would like to be this way, too. To produce these results requires redesigning the game they play. We have to create a culture that liberates each of us to collaborate, create, and contribute.

Here's a window into a different kind of culture: a leadership culture. Notice how some of the behaviors in this educational culture (a) are uncommon in "real life," and (b) could be quite functional, if we got practiced in them.

Most of all, we need to upgrade our understanding of children.

CHAPTER 2

Thank You for Criticizing

Criticism is an essential design element of Andre Perry's class of fourth and fifth graders. Andre designed it so that the students would educate each other.

Each week the students had to learn nine words. Andre gave them the words on Monday. They looked them up, learned the definitions, and used them in sentences. They came to know these words—in some cases intimately—as they discussed their different meanings in class and the different roles they can play in sentences. By Thursday, when Mathias, a substitute teacher, taught the class, they had each written a story using all nine words.

Mathias didn't so much teach as preside, as the students took turns standing in the center of the room, all poised and proud, reading their pieces. After each one, the hands went up. Here are some of their comments:

"I really liked the story. I mean, it's a real story. I would like to learn more about the character. The only word that seemed forced was 'communism.'"

"That was a very nice piece. I want to know what happens. I think you should finish it—I mean not for homework—just, you know, finish it."

"I liked the efficient way you used 'tragedy' and 'catastrophe' right at the beginning by using them dramatically."

"Yes, that was good, but we are supposed to use them so that it is obvious what they mean from the way we use them, and I don't think tone of voice counts."

"It has a good plot; I am interested; I want to know more. But the part about 'rural' and 'urban'—that seemed just stuck in there."

The students were so organized that in half an hour we had read and criticized five stories and one poem. The class almost ran itself. The only thing

Mathias "taught" was: "When you use 'but' in giving criticism, it erases the part of your sentence that comes before it. Say it again using 'and.'"

Mathias was impressed both by their disciplined approach to literature and by the quality of their talk. Criticism seemed to strengthen rather than hurt their relationships. Defensiveness reared its ugly head only once and then only slightly and quickly corrected. One of the last comments was from someone who hadn't had a chance to read: "This is for everyone. We were supposed to take nine very hard words."

"Only seven were really hard," interrupted a friend.

"Yes, seven hard ones," he continued, "and force them into a story. It was really good—well, like, we couldn't tell that you were doing that. They all sounded like real stories. I couldn't tell that it was an assignment."

He was observing that his classmates had done two things at once—learn the words and write from the heart.

Andre's design concept was to teach not as if some of them might be authors some day. Instead, he taught as if all of them were already authors and that giving and receiving criticism is an essential educational objective. Of course. To become a good writer you have to get good at giving and receiving criticism.

But criticism isn't just important in writing. If making good decisions requires an accurate perception of reality, then criticism is essential for all human endeavors. If we want to make something good, do anything well, or have good relationships, we have to get good at giving and receiving criticism.

What are the key design elements of cultures that support criticism? Andre's class shows us some of the assumptions that underlie his design:

1. To maximize achievement, focus on learning rather than achievement.
2. Truth and beauty are achieved through a process of collective successive approximation.
3. Useful creativity springs from relationships.
4. If you want to get them thinking, ask them what *they* think.
5. Talk to kids the same way you talk to adults.
6. Use descriptive language and insist on it in others. Don't label.
7. Allow difficult conversations; get good at talking about hard things.
8. Remember your job is to increase *their* authority, not yours.
9. Changing your mind is a good thing.
10. Arrogance, perfection, and defensiveness are learning disabilities.
11. Delivering feedback that is hearable, seeable, and doable requires continual practice.

12. Mistakes, difference, and conflict are welcomed as opportunities to learn.
13. We are all imperfect. Everyone comes pre-forgiven.

We may not insist that our kids grow up to be authors, but we do want them to be authorities, authorities who have good working relationships with other authorities, authorities who never stop learning, and the foundation for this is the truth. The more we distort reality or collude in distorting reality, the weaker the relationship, the weaker the team, and therefore, the weaker the results.

Trustworthy authorities know, and know they don't know, both at the same time. Being an authority that people respect includes putting learning first—always dedicated to exposing the gap between what we think we know and the truth. To be authorities we must be as interested in what we did wrong as what we did right.

Being an authority that people respect includes more than just knowing. An educated person is skilled at thinking abstractly and communicating concretely, thinking creatively and applying it practically. Good schools normally take responsibility for these skills. But often, even these same schools don't take much responsibility for other important skillsets: working with others, making conflicts creative, setting goals and mastering one's self, and contributing to the well-being of others.

Deficits in these areas are blamed on bad parenting, or genetic disabilities, or "the family," or poverty. "Twenty-First-Century Skills" is what they are being called today.

In activities of ever-increasing complexity, we are all challenged to develop these skills whether we like it or not—in case you hadn't noticed, this is what it means to be alive and human—but the delivery system for these skills is culture. Andre Perry's class is an example of what it looks like and how it works.

Real authority is a function of relationships. If a person writes a book and no one reads it does it exist? If a person knows what is true or knows what to do in a social vacuum is there authority? To be effective we must be authorities-in-relationship so that our authority will bring out authority in others and improve the quality of the larger organism that is our group. Leadership is exercising authority for positive impact. Effective leaders lead through partnership. For best results, partnership delivers the outcome.

Delivering criticism that can be heard, and learning from any criticism however badly delivered, is essential to this enterprise. This is what it means to be educated. In fact, criticizing so as to build rather than hurt relationships is the secret to a happy and successful life.

The negative connotations of "criticize" show how challenging it is to surface the truth. Other people might not want to hear your criticism or won't be able to understand what you are talking about or won't be able to put it into practice. We may not be able to deliver criticism because we are afraid we will hurt others' feelings and thus hurt the relationship. We might not be able to deliver the message so that the other person will understand what we are saying. We might say it in such a way that they end up doing exactly the wrong thing in response.

These are the challenges of being human. Succeeding at this enterprise day by day requires practicing some disciplines. Many of these disciplines are hard for us. We humans naturally avoid mistakes, failure, conflict, and strangeness even though we know that challenges like mistakes, failure, conflict, and strangeness are where most of our important learnings come from.

The social environments we create can make practicing and learning these disciplines easier or harder. Because we are social animals, our behavior is powerfully affected by the social context in which we make our decisions. Our natural tendency to avoid embarrassment and conflict can lead us into a host of learning disabilities.

Andre's twenty fourth and fifth graders were not particularly special kids. They had spent a few years in a school environment that respected them as learners, as people who care about others as whole human beings, as people who are dedicated to making a difference. Above all they had grown up in a social environment where everybody matters. Noticing what works for children has given me clues as to what we adults need in order to create creative environments that maximize learning, grow authority, and produce leaders for a better world.

Knowing the key elements of learning cultures is one thing. Creating them is another. One of the themes running through portraits of great educational cultures is conflict. Humans are always in conflict or incipient conflict with each other because we are different—unique. Building criticism into the culture of an organization as a habit is a critical design element of a learning organization.

Andre focused his genius on the genius in each of his students; thus, he snuck past all their normal tendencies for defensiveness, competition, peer pressure, and conformity.

By contrast Graham's school didn't.

CHAPTER 3

Arrogance Is a Learning Disability

To live is the rarest thing in the world. Most people exist, that is all.

—Oscar Wilde

"Fuck you" was written in red crayon on the painting of a second grader, and Amy was called into the headmaster's office.

The ruined work of art was hanging in the hallway of the main school building among dozens of other pieces that the art teacher had decided were exemplary.

Amy had been hired the day before as a consultant for the school's "Kind Kids Count" program, an initiative that had grown out of a faculty meeting a year ago. Students were mean to each other; put-downs were a common currency of social interaction; competition for the right answer in class caused them to cut each other off in mid-speech. Bullying, cheating, and intimidation were rife. On the sports field and basketball court, competitiveness had gone mean. Teacher frustration was high, and "Kind Kids Count" was not working.

Finding the culprit and punishing him was not what the headmaster wanted Amy to do; he was completely capable of doing that himself, and indeed, before the week was out the perpetrator had been identified, and appropriate consequences had been meted out.

The headmaster and Amy were both clear on the concept that bullying was a symptom of a deeper problem, a problem that was built into the culture of the school. He wanted help identifying the cultural culprit.

On Amy's seventh visit to the school a moment occurred that brought her to the heart of the matter. She happened into the teacher's lounge one day as a group of teachers were discussing seventh grader Graham. Their frustration showed in the intensity of their conversation.

"He is, also, downright mean to his classmates," said the art teacher. "Fernando's mother was complaining to me about him last week."

"I know," said the English teacher. "Today, in homeroom we were talking about meanness. You know what Graham said? He said, 'People should just suck it up and deal.'"

"He's a bully," blurted the art teacher.

Amy had met Graham and watched him in class. She had even tried to teach a class he was in. Graham's hand was always the first up, but he didn't wait to be called on. He interrupted, talked over people, intimidated to make his point, and used sarcasm liberally. He rarely acted as if he was learning, but rather proving he was the smartest.

"Let's face it. He's arrogant," said one teacher.

"With a father like that, what do you expect?" said another.

"Yeah, but the thing is he is such a good student," said the algebra teacher.

Then, Amy spoke up. "But arrogance is a learning disability," she said.

There was laughter in the lounge.

"We laugh," she said, "but the funny thing is that it's true. Graham is at risk, and we are not saying so. Instead we are calling him a good student."

"But *he* is a good student," said the English teacher. "He's getting straight A's. How can you say he is at risk?"

"What does it mean to be a good student?" she asked. "Is a good student the one who is good at getting the right answers or the one who learns the most?"

"I know what you mean, but come on," said his algebra teacher. "When you get straight A's you are a great student."

"Wait. That statement is oxymoronic. Arrogance is a learning disability. He may get good grades on tests, but he is inhibiting his own learning as well as others. A know-it-all will not learn as much as someone who will listen to others," Amy said. "Graham is showing us that there is something wrong with our grading system. An A-student would be asking questions, listening to others, building on their ideas and striving to understand, rather than trying to impress everyone else with how much he already knows.

"Okay, so he gets A's all the way through college, did he benefit from his parents' enormous investment? For kids to benefit from college, they have to be learners. Sooner or later, the know-it-alls run into trouble." She paused. "And we will never get his father to help us help him change if we label him a 'strong student.' That's what his father is going for."

"Are you saying if we change the report card, he will stop being mean to people?" asked the math teacher?

"No, but that might be a good first step."

"That's crazy," said Graham's homeroom teacher.

"What's crazy is doing the same thing and expecting to get the different results. The grading system is connected to the disciplinary system, the awards ceremony at the end of the year . . . everything. Every piece of what we do here is intimately connected to every other piece." . . . the conversation went on without resolution. It was only a conversation in a faculty lounge.

From a distance we all know that arrogance is a leadership disability as well as a learning disability. Arrogance is the root of tyranny, and we know the disasters that tyranny can cause both in and out of school. Whether Chairman of the Federal Reserve or intern at an investment bank, experienced CEO or rookie computer programmer, head of school or teacher, friend or spouse, those who are arrogant, indeed, have a learning disability that will compromise their leadership, their mission, their success as well as their happiness, not only in seventh grade but throughout life.

Arrogance has caused the failure of companies and has been the downfall of kingdoms. Arrogance has caused people to lose their friends, their spouses, their jobs, and even their heads (both literally and figuratively.)

Leading and learning go hand in hand. The Latin *educare* means "to lead out." Educators lead each person's character out into the world to contribute constructively, creatively, and gracefully to it. The measure of effective education is the degree to which it brings out the leadership in others. Educators are authorities trying to increase the authority of their students. Authoritarian authorities are trying to maximize the opposite.

On one level we all know this, but in real life we are not surprised by arrogance. We have come to expect it. We are not surprised because we see it all around us and take it for granted, and we take it for granted because we are all bound up in the culture that makes arrogant actions good moves in what seems to be the game of life.

"Some people are just that way," we say by way of distancing ourselves from this world, but we can't really distance ourselves, because we are all caught up in it. If we are honest with ourselves we see ourselves getting sucked into our own habitual set of behaviors that have allowed us to cope with this kind of social environment.

Graham was not born arrogant. His disability was created by the context he grew up in, a culture in which his school was entirely complicit. In this culture, independence is a core value, not interdependence. The idea that

Graham has as much to learn from "those other dummies" as they could learn from him rarely occurs to anyone.

Like most schools, Graham's school is still operating as if *knowing* is what education is all about. The school's mission statement says, "We graduate leaders," but in reality, it graduates lemmings. Graham's school is more of an achievement mill than a leadership community, and the necessary ingredients for creativity are missing.

The culture Graham grows up in shapes his brain.

Across the country, most schools have created their own kind of achievement mill. Whether the school is public or private, and regardless of the socio-economic status of the families, regardless of the neighborhood, most schools are designed so that everyone plays *The Pyramid Game*. The culture is constructed to sort them into more or less likely to succeed.

From the report card to the "Awards Ceremony" at the end of the year, their structures are designed to sort for "natural leaders" rather than to educate them all to be leaders. The way to rise up the pyramid is simple: maximize right answers and minimize being wrong. You show you're smart by telling; asking shows you're stupid. Looking out for yourself is the law of the land. As Graham said, "People should just need to suck it up and deal."

This social context does not turn out the kind of people we would like to have leading us. This kind of leadership will not increase the creativity in our organizations—in fact it constrains creativity.

In addition to arrogance, comparison to others, obsession with ability, fearing diversity, avoidance of responsibility, underestimating the natural generosity of others, needing to control the outcome of our decisions and the flow of information, failure to see others as assets, and the need to save face are all disabilities. Some environments exacerbate these tendencies, and when they do, a great deal of psychic energy goes into these distractions rather than collaborating, creating, and contributing.

By contrast, when a culture is built on the assumption of our imperfection, the assumption that everyone is building their character and that all characters are in search of their own unique way to contribute, then all that psychic energy can go into becoming the unique, authoritative individuals that we are meant to become.

When we are not trying to measure up or placate or fit in or hide, we can take on challenges, make and learn from mistakes, practice the disciplines of turning conflict into collaboration and friendship, and take the risks necessary to create great moments. Great schools can be excellent laboratories for learning the design elements of such cultures, because all this is often easier for children than it is for adults.

CHAPTER 4

In Education, Failure Is an Option

New Myths for Successful Kids and Better Schools

Success is failing again and again without losing enthusiasm.

—Winston Churchill

In Education, failure IS an option, and a pretty good one at that.

Fear of failure is not a big issue for most kids going off to first grade. Their life is not yet framed with questions of success and failure. Even after a year in kindergarten where their mission was to make friends, do fun things, and learn as much as they can, the concept of failure isn't really on the brain, much.

Unfortunately, most schools try to change this. Our culture is obsessed with success and failure in the context of a pyramid model of society, where a few will make it to the top and many will be left at the bottom. In our schools, this obsession generates a number of myths which result in (surprise, surprise) a few winners, many losers, and a lot of mediocrity. A few people will become self-disciplined, self-critical learners who are comfortable in their own skin, good at working with others, and practiced in thinking creatively. The majority will fall short and handle their inadequacies as best they can.

At the level of national policy both "No Child Left Behind" and "The Race to the Top" are (obviously) trapped inside the pyramid—right along with the rest of us. National and local education policies are powered by the same myths that drive with us to school every day. Myths like:

Chapter 4

> Nothing succeeds like success.
> Life is a race to the top of a pyramid.
> Academic achievement is the ticket to the top.
> The race starts in kindergarten with kids at ZERO.
> Academics skills are a good measure of your intelligence.
> Struggling with an academic problem signals you are not smart.
> There are three kinds of kids: gifted, average, those who learn differently.
> To achieve success you must lead with your strengths and hide your weaknesses.
> Parents have the power to get their children to turn out the way they want them to.
> Education is about shaping your child and getting your child through an eye of a needle.
> You must sacrifice imagination, curiosity, and your soul to get through the eye of the needle.

Worst of all, because academics is something you wouldn't naturally like, you therefore have to sacrifice your imagination, your inquisitiveness, and your self to get through the eye of the needle.

None of these folktales are borne out either by experience or research. Nothing succeeds like grit. Nothing succeeds like courage, connecting with people, mastering collaboration, and confidence in that peculiar combination of strengths and weaknesses that make you your own weird self. In other words, the kindergarteners have it right in the first place. If they come out of school screwed up, it is a pyramid school with parental support that screwed them up.

Actually, one of these myths is, arguably, true. Which one? (turn the page)

Right. You *can* get a head start by starting the race early. It is true that early environment has a powerful effect on brain development, but getting an early start on academics can actually hurt. Don't start the race early. Raising your child in a complex environment builds a more complex brain, but seeing it as race and comparing your child with others to see how ahead or behind they are, weakens them. Even in a race, looking over your shoulder slows you down.

Although ingrained in our minds like bad habits, these myths vanish in the face of a little conversation between parents and teachers about children in the absence of fear. A little reminding and people can usually refocus on what matters.

1. Nothing succeeds like success.

No, as Winston Churchill said: Success is failing again and again without losing enthusiasm.

2. Life is a race to the top of some pyramid.

No, it's not. "I have arrived" is a mirage. Living is growing. For learners there is more and more opportunity as we get older, not less and less. It is best to focus children on pursuing their calling, developing their character, building a self, making a difference. Put learning first and achievement will follow.

3. Academic achievement is the ticket to the top (test scores/brand name colleges).

No. Academic achievement is a ticket to academic achievement. People hire confident learners who can work with others. Academic achievement is only one measure of that, and smart employers know that it is not a very good one.

4. The race starts in kindergarten with kids at ZERO.

Not at all. By the time they walk into their first kindergarten classroom and are asked to sit in a circle, children have already been researchers, scientists, detectives, and problem-solvers for over forty-three-thousand hours. Treat them as if they already know a lot and are passionate about learning more.

5. Academics are a good measure of your intelligence.

Wrong. Only a certain kind of intelligence.

6. Struggling with an academic problem signals you are not smart.

Wrong. The truth is there are many kinds of intelligence, and there is no correlation between academic prowess and any measure of happiness or adult effectiveness. But the myth sets people up for failure and unhappiness. Research on happiness shows that there is no correlation between position on the pyramid and happiness. Connection to Others, Work that you Love, Loving to Learn. This is success. One more thing: Loving a challenge. The habit of learning from disappointment, failure, loss, mistakes, conflict, newness, and so on are the predictors of success. Pain is a necessary ingredient of all lives regardless of how "high" you are on the mythical pyramid.

7. It is all about ability, and there are three kinds of kids: gifted, normal, and those who learn differently.

We know that is not true. We each learn differently, have a unique set of gifts and talents, and none of us is "normal." Ability is something we can develop depending upon what we commit to do and practice. Kids maintain a growth mindset (if you practice, you'll get smarter) when they are free from labels of themselves—good or bad. Be great, not excellent. Don't compare yourself with others. "Best" distracts us from being great because it allows the notion of comparison to creep in. Don't label.

8. To achieve success, you must lead with your strengths; hide your weaknesses.

No. Success comes from finding work that you love and bringing your whole self to the table.

9. Parents have the power to get their kids to turn out the way they want them to.

No. Parents have influence. But children come into the world as their own people, and our job is to help them be that person more effectively and gracefully. A child is not some sort of project in which we can control the outcome. A parent's power is limited. The three ways we can have a positive effect is (1) treat them as decision makers, (2) clarify and defend boundaries, and (3) provide unconditional love. Love them and tell them the truth.

10. Similarly, education is about shaping your child or a bit like getting your child through the eye of the needle.

No. As with parents, when schools try to shape children, the children come out misshapen. Education is leading a person's character out into the world to contribute effectively, creatively, and gracefully to it. Drop "getting ahead" or "being behind." Help each child learn the skills they need to master real challenges.

11. You have to sacrifice your imagination, your inquisitiveness, and your self to get through the eye of the needle to the next level of academic achievement.

On the contrary, imagination, inquisitiveness, integrity, grit, enthusiasm, inspiration, practice, perseverance, courage, resilience, and so on are the key disciplines of development of character and also the key elements of academic success. Fulfillment of self and mastering academic standards go hand in hand.

These myths will die as more and more schools embrace the new era. My agony is that meanwhile our society is breaking in two. Millions of people are getting an education, but tens of millions are not, and many of those without parental or community support are being cast onto the discard pile of our rapidly changing world.

Many of those who feel that the system is rigged against them, blame the wrong system and support authoritarian tyrants.

The children do not start off trapped. Success and failure are adult concepts, and wise educators don't entertain them. Certainly, there are a few children with *bona fide* neurological disabilities, but virtually all children can read, all children can learn to control their impulses and focus, and all children can be good at mathematics. The vast majority of those labeled disabled acquire the label because they didn't reveal themselves capable according to the (time-honored) timetable established by school. By fourth grade the sorting is mostly complete, and we are pretty sure who is normal, who is gifted, and who "learns differently."

What if "learning differences" were a concept honored and embedded in a system of education that was striving for what all kindergartners are originally striving for—to make something of their wonderful imperfect selves. They are in the process of discovering their gifts and none of them are "normal."

Whether or not these alternative statements are "TRUE" is off the subject. The point is that when people in a community act as if they are true, the community is more likely to produce an educated citizenry and a much larger number of happy, successful people than the myths of the pyramid model.

As we send our kids off to school, we should not wish for them success. We should not envision their hands in the air dying to be called on so they can give the right answer time after time. We should not hope that their classroom is peopled with all friends and no bullies. We don't send our kids to school for it to be easy; we should want it to be hard. What would be the point of easy?

Of course, we parents want our children to be happy and successful. But parents can give their kids neither. Self-confidence derives not from success or praise but from experiencing yourself as someone who can "meet with triumph and disaster" and come out stronger, smarter, and wiser.

Here is my blessing for all the children in school this year:

May you develop the grit to live in life's tensions, the confidence to learn from conflict, mistakes, disappointment, failure, loneliness, and losing, and the skills to find the fun in every day and the love in every person. In the process may you never fall out of love with learning.

CHAPTER 5

Measure What Matters

"The truth is, everyone is going to hurt you. You just got to find the ones worth suffering for."

—Bob Marley

In October of 1988 at St. Paul's Episcopal School in Oakland, California, Edie, the new Middle School English teacher couldn't sleep. She had a dilemma. Some students were working hard and kept getting bad grades, and others got good grades without really trying.

One day while her students were at recess she talked to Karen, the math teacher, about her concern and discovered that she had the same concern. "Yes, Sara is a model student," she said, "but she keeps failing her math tests. I am afraid she going to get an F."

"Sara gets good grades in English, but I have other kids I am concerned about," and thus began a running conversation that resulted in the two of them coming to see me. We had a month before the first progress reports had to go out.

When Edie and Karen came to my office Karen's opening line was: "We don't want to be guilty of grade inflation, but the grading system isn't fair. Sara, for instance, works really hard. She always does her homework and participates in class. She is actually a great student, but she is math-phobic. She keeps failing her tests. We don't know what to do."

I asked, "Well, you say she is a great student. What does that look like? What does 'participates in class' look like?"

"She's just great at working with others."

"Yes, but what does that look like? If we can describe it, we can measure it, if we can measure it, we can grade it."

"Well, she builds on other people's ideas . . ."

". . . and she asks good questions, and well, it's her attitude . . ."

"But what does a great attitude look like?"

We decided to include the whole faculty in the discussion, and two meetings later we had a new report card. (If you think you'll change the culture of your school without changing the report card, you don't understand the situation.) We decided to give two grades—one for "Learning," another for "Mastery"—and average them. Sara might get "F" in mastery, "A" in learning, and a "C" for the course. To be rigorous we picked ten observable behaviors and named them "Disciplines of a Learner:"

1. Speaks up
2. Listens with an openness to change
3. Welcomes a challenge
4. Uses mistakes as learning opportunities
5. Takes risks
6. Takes criticism constructively
7. Perseveres in tasks
8. Asks questions
9. Builds on other people's ideas
10. Knows when to lead and when to follow.

Graded on a four-point scale of 4 = consistently, 3 = often, 2 = sometimes, 1 = rarely, students could set goals to improve their learning.

Problem solved. And of course, Sara started getting Bs with no grade inflation, because she could see that her learning, not her intelligence, mattered. (And as Stanford professor *Carol Dweck* would predict, her intelligence actually grew.)[1]

Furthermore, the high schools loved the transcript because they were given more information about what lay behind a B− or a C+. They began reporting back that they loved our graduates because they were leaders. When students felt they could control their own progress toward success, the whole middle school took another giant step toward being a learning community.

BEING A LEADER IS SIMPLY THE MARK OF BEING EDUCATED.

These "Skills of a Learner" are the same as the skills needed for being a good leader. If you want to get good at defining yourself to a challenging situation, you need to master this set of skills, for being a leader is simply the mark of being educated. Should an arrogant student be considered an excellent student with this grading system? Education is essentially anti-tyranny training.

Helping each person learn how to take a stand justly, how to listen with a willingness to learn, how to stand up to others with Truth, how to lead gracefully, how to bring all the disparate forces in our communities into harmony, how to bring all the disparate forces in ourselves to integrity and wholeness—at the core of all these enterprises is the idea that each of us has a genius and that our geniuses are in league with each other.

Tyrants present us with these challenges, and rising to these challenges is not only the job of an educator or "leader," but also the job of anyone who wants to lead a good life. These skills are manifestations of a well-educated person, a person who is self-actualizing, and none of this can be accomplished without being in touch with your inner teacher.

If we want to create a culture for learning and leading, we have to measure what matters. Without holding people accountable for practicing these skills, people in an organization default to driving straight for the "measurable outcomes" (test scores, college acceptances, ROI, the stock price, etc.) Giving lip service to being thoughtful of others and measuring only mastery, communicates that being thoughtful of others doesn't really matter.

If an organization has only a few measures of success, then winning at their game looks hopeless for some, and they take other paths—some that are destructive.

Several years ago, Tony Wagner started asking CEO's: "Which qualities will our graduates need in the twenty-first century for success in college, careers, and citizenship?" Over six-hundred interviews later he published his list of *Seven Survival Skills* in *The Global Achievement Gap* (Basic Books 2010):[2]

- Critical thinking and problem-solving
- Collaboration across networks and leading by influence
- Agility and adaptability
- Initiative and entrepreneurship
- Effective oral and written communication
- Accessing and analyzing information
- Curiosity and imagination

In *Mind in the Making* (Harper Collins 2010), Ellen Galinsky presents "The Seven Essential Life Skills Every Child Needs." Looking at the Table of Contents you can't argue. If we were hiring—for whatever occupation—we would want someone who could (1) focus and control themselves, (2) take other perspectives, (3) make connections, (4) communicate, (5) think critically, (6) take on challenges, and (7) love learning.[3]

Whether you are playing four-square on the playground or working with a partner in the science lab, whether you are a salesperson or the marketing director of a corporation, an administrator or an administrative assistant, these skills are essential. If you were looking for partners for a project, you would want them to have these abilities. As Galinsky points out these seven skills are the functions of the prefrontal cortex, the decision-making center of our brain, the core of our reality-testing mechanism.

By now, many people have gotten on board with the idea and have generated their own lists of "soft skills," or "non-cognitive skills" and everyone seems to understand that we all need them today—so much so that we are all talking about "Twenty-First Century learning skills," and everyone seems to have their own list. They are now a central part of the conversation about what should be going on in schools.

This is progress. At last, educators and policy makers are in sync with what parents have long known we want for our children. I have evolved my own: concentrate, collaborate, connect, communicate, criticize, create, and contribute. If our children had these skills sets, what would be missing? Skills for academic achievement, skills for leadership, and skills for life are essentially the same set of skills.

But the cultures of most schools—even rich schools with good reputations—are imprisoned in antique concepts, and our language proves it. "Soft skills" and "non-cognitive skills" are misnomers.

First, they are not "non-cognitive," but highly cognitive. Secondly, there is nothing "soft" about them. They are hard, and you have to be hard-nosed to use them. Thirdly, there is nothing new about them. Teachers have always cared about them. In this age's obsession with "hard data" until we call it "the Hard Curriculum" and put it first on the report card, we will keep failing to get these results.

This would mean that teachers would be responsible for doing what got them into education in the first place: focusing on educating the whole brain, focusing on the child's self-actualization every day, creating the conditions in which children learn to be respectful leaders with a sense of social responsibility, making sure that all the children in every class leave school every day feeling worthy, efficacious, and competent.

If our mission is to graduate leaders, people who face up to conflict, take stands, and learn from their mistakes, people who can speak up and listen at the same time, this mission needs to be woven into the fabric of our schools, and our language will have to change along with it.

This would mean that administrators are held accountable for empowering the teachers: guiding them through challenging relationships, helping them over humps, reminding them of why they are here in the first place. Holding teachers accountable for covering the curriculum and reporting scores on standardized tests? What menial tasks. How insulting. No wonder the teaching profession is not held in high esteem in our society.

What if school didn't *prepare* you for something, but prepared you for *anything*? Imagine progress reports that grade only concentrates, collaborates, connects, communicates, criticizes, creates, and contributes on a four point scale: Consistently (4), Often (3), Sometimes (2), Rarely (1)? Since high scores in these items would predict success in whatever a person endeavored, maybe employers would actually ask to see a report card. If teachers taught to this test, they would be doing their job.

Edie and Karen showed us the kind of leadership necessary to get this job done.

CHAPTER 6

The Culture We Create Is Visible in Everything We Do

"Mom, I'm just wasting my time. I can't read, I can't write, and they won't let me talk!"

—Five-year-old Ellie after her first week of school.

When Cooperative Learning Groups Do the Teaching

Several years after the faculty redesigned the report card at St. Paul's, a visitor to Matt Ronfeldt's eighth-grade algebra class would probably witness something like the following scene if she came at the end of his ninety-minute class.

Twenty-four students seated four-to-a-table talking with great animation about the algebra problems in front of them. Matt would be moving among the tables with a clipboard. Fifteen minutes before they broke for lunch, Matt says something like, "Great work everyone. I was thrilled with how you were working together. Here's some feedback for you."

"Mikaela, you exercised leadership when you asked, 'Wait. What are we solving for?'"

"Danielle, remember when you stopped arguing and just wrote down what you thought the answer was and slipped it across the table to the others? Notice how that shifted the conversation?"

"Taharka, three times I saw you take someone else's idea and build on it."

"Table 4, I love how you each seemed to know when to speak and when to listen."

"Okay, close your eyes for a minute. Go back over the last half hour, think of how you worked together. Remember leadership moments. [pause] Okay, think of who did the most listening. [pause] Got it? When I say 'Go' open your eyes and point to who did the most listening."

Matt would go on like that till lunch giving each student feedback on how they exercised leadership. The students were learning algebra; Matt was teaching leadership, and everyone had been a leader at one time or another.

Can we teach social responsibility and academics at the same time? Yes, in fact we must. Teaching social responsibility as a separate subject is, to the kids, a joke. It's like teaching an artist to paint by the numbers. Seventh graders have been building their social brains for over one-hundred-thousand hours before they walk into their first algebra class.

It should be no surprise to us that children are so socially competent. We humans acquired our large brains, because one branch of the primate line started to get serious about collaborating. There is good research to supporting the hypothesis that our large brains are a result of social problem solving of which building a sophisticated language is a subset.

If we want them to do better, we need to design the game they are playing so that it produces these results. Schools that teach children as if they are already experts at many aspects of learning, get better results. Parents would be happier with their children if they understood their children for the social scientists they are.

Matt is showing us how.

When the Awards Ceremony Celebrates the Unique Contributions of Each Graduate

All schools have to care about academic achievement, test scores, and getting to the next level of schooling successfully. But as with many things, the aim must be different from the goal. In golf, for instance, the best way to put the ball in the cup is to concentrate, not on the cup, but on your swing. As with golf: focusing on being the best takes our eye off the ball of learning.

Two years after we changed our report card, we changed our award ceremony, and the process of change was like the process for changing the report card.

Again, two middle-school teachers came to my office three weeks before graduation and said, "We hate the awards ceremony. We are sitting there trying to decide who is the Best Citizen, the Top Student, the Best Athlete, and who should get the Leadership Award, and we hate it."

"It's not that we are worried about hurting anyone's feelings," said Matt "or their (he made air quotes with his fingers) 'self-esteem.' It's that it's not true. All year long we have been striving to have every student be their own kind of great student. Now we have to say who won."

Then Nancy spoke up: "Everyone actually IS a good citizen in their own way. I mean no one's perfect, but we don't want it to be the goody-goody award."

"And that's true for Leadership as well," added Matt.

"Sure, some kids are better athletes than others—some are just not athletes—but we don't want to single out one person—it's an integrity issue—it's just not true."

"And the Progress Award," said Nancy. "That's the worst. It is the award "given to that student who, in the opinion of the faculty, has grown the most that year." Aren't we trying to make it so everyone grows? Besides, the "Progress Award" is universally known by students to be the "Dummy Award."

"I get it," I said. "It is the reward for learning, and nobody wants it."

I went to the middle school meeting to talk about it, and it was interesting; they all agreed. But I said, "No. We can't just eliminate a ritual. We have to replace it with something that is obviously better. Changing a ritual is not something we do like changing our coat. Rituals and symbols are built into our culture. We only have three weeks, and making this kind of change takes a little time, because have to bring people along."

They were upset with me, but next year, we talked about it in January. I said, "I know. I actually agree. From the day our children entered kindergarten, we told them that learning was the goal—and then at the end of their nine years with us, we give one award for achievement. Every day, we celebrate the unique genius of each child—but then at graduation, we say who's *the* genius. But what are we going to replace it with?"

The teachers had come to the meeting prepared. They had been talking about it off and on since last spring. They presented their plan. They said that each of them, including all the specialist teachers, would take a few students and each one would say one moment of greatness about each student. In the process, of course, they would be covering areas of citizenship, academics, creativity, physical education, leadership, and so on. All the adults who had had contact with the eighth graders would be involved. Each would write one or two sentences about a moment of greatness and read these messages at graduation.

I said I would talk to the Board about it and get their blessing. I did the same with the Parents' Association. Getting the rest of the community talking about it was essential. We all needed to get educated, not just the educators.

To make several conversations short, we did change, and at the end of the year, each student's success is enthusiastically celebrated by the entire school community.

Changing the ritual helped to change the culture, too. Its effects are felt all year long as each student uses his or her own passion, integrity, and inspiration as criteria for measuring success.

By Contrast: What Is the Game These Students Are Playing?

A large suburban K-12 school in the Midwest is considered to be one of the best schools in the area. "Everyone wants their children to go there" because it is the best path to the top of the pyramid. Yes, there were cliques, bullies and "mean girls," but well, isn't that just kids being kids?

Touring the school in December, you come at a time of year when the seniors are caught up in the anxiety of working on their college applications. When your tour guide leads you into the high school hallway, she points at the lockers that lined the hallway and says with pride, "These are the senior lockers. You can tell that some of the seniors have already received their college acceptances. By tradition, when a student is accepted at a college, they put the pennant of that college on their locker. These students were accepted 'early decision.'"

Indeed, one locker has a Princeton pennant; another one has a Harvard pennant and so on. About a dozen lockers are sporting a flag bragging about the colleges that certain students had already been accepted to. Is this an environment that will maximize student performance? Research shows that it doesn't even maximize the performance of those who got Ivy League pennants on their lockers.

People don't maximize their performance when they are anxiously comparing themselves to others. They maximize their performance when their anxiety is low and they are focusing on building themselves. When they practice speaking up, asking questions, making a difference to others, pursuing goals that are meaningful to them, solving problems, resolving conflicts, making mistakes, learning and leading, they are increasing their chances of success.

The same is true for social climate. In "Bully-Proofing Kids" Michele Borba details about sixty things that parents can do to combat bullying. But these are coping mechanisms. To bully-proof schools we must change the culture, and to change the culture, we have to measure what matters. When kids are on a meaningful mission, bullying just doesn't enter in—conflict yes, but bullying, no. When a classmate falters and gets mean, there are others who stand strong and lead him/her back to better ways.

Concerned about the behavior among students, many schools institute "Character Education" programs. In these programs, the word character really means morality. "Character traits" are taught as any academic subject, students roll their eyes at their morality classes, and immoral behavior continues unabated. They are well aware of the discontinuity between the morality that is being taught and the social behaviors that are built into the culture of their school.

When the school focuses on self-actualization, we get everything we want: strong, self-directed people who are also good at getting along with others, which includes, of course, a high incidence of moral behavior. Whether a student is searching for the right words to address a classmate or the best way to state a thesis in an essay, the challenge is essentially the same. Collecting oneself before entering the exam room, the sports arena, or the playground requires the same disciplines. The skills for solving math problems and social problems overlap.

Educating "the whole person" starts with understanding that our work is to fully educate each character in our care. Humility, perseverance, openness, courage, patience, creativity, integrity, resourcefulness, kindness, generosity, and forgiveness: We call them virtues and talk about them as if they were "traits" of character. And it is perhaps true that these skills are easier for some people than others, but this point of view points to powerlessness.

Acting as if these "virtues" are disciplines, skills that help us accomplish our goals, skills that we can develop through practice, is an essential ingredient for building character. Understanding that these disciplines serve us well in all endeavors from the social to the academic, from the artistic to the athletic, helps the culture we are in become more and more the way we want it.

The habit of taking responsibility is necessary for both homework and interpersonal conflict. The habit of always being respectful no matter what is essential for collaborating both in and out of the classroom. Respect and taking responsibility, like other disciplines, are not character traits, but skills that can be learned. Until everyone understands that education of character is education itself, schools will have little impact on making a positive difference in our individual lives or our collective lives.

What do we have to do so that Ellie and her four million classmates get an education? In my experience, it only takes a few people. One person speaks from her soul, and the souls of couple of others build on that leadership, and change begins. And yes, it sure helps if the establishment is a learning organization, but in any case, Ellie can always say something like: "The Emperor has no clothes."

CHAPTER 7

First-Grade Teacher Designs a Learning Organization

The best way to predict your future is to create it.

—Peter F. Drucker

> Warning: requires continual maintenance. If you need to be perfect, are conflict-averse, are afraid of failure, or are so good and experienced that you are "not about to change," do not try this without professional assistance.

Design a learning organization in one hour in your classroom, school, business, or backyard. A first-grade teacher, James, shows us how.

First thing on the first day of a new school year, James gathers his class of twenty-four students into a circle on the floor of the classroom. He launches the new year with:

(Mission)
"I am sitting here with you because I love learning."
"I love teaching, because the more I teach, the more I learn. The more I learn the smarter and happier I get."
"My hope for you all is that by the end of the year you feel the same way I do."
"SO, this year is going to be the best learning year ever."

(Strategy)
"Humans tend to learn best in groups. We learn more, and we learn better, when we learn with and from each other. That's why there's school."

"How much we learn has a lot to do with how much we enjoy it, and how much we enjoy it has to do with how well organized we are as a learning team."

"So, let's get organized. Together, we are going to build an awesome learning organization."

(Design)

Standing in front of an easel with poster-size Post-its James says: "How can other people help you learn?" and writes down their answers.

The class comes up with a list like:
Ask if they can help me,
Asks me what the problem is,
Listens to me,
Doesn't get mad at me,
Shows me how,
Asks good questions,
Is friendly,
Doesn't talk too much,
Asks me to help them, . . . sometimes.

[N. B. Depending on how new this idea is to the students, the initial list will be more or less rudimentary. The purpose of creating a starter list is to get them thinking about what it takes to build a learning community. The quality of the initial list doesn't matter, because it will grow and improve in the course of the year.]

(The Plan)

Then James says: "Great start. We have made a starter list of the disciplines of a learning organization; if we do these things we will all learn a lot. Now, here's how we build our organization."

Going to his desk where a bowl of green marbles stands next to a pretty, empty jar labeled "Learning Bank," he says: "Every time you see someone do something that helps someone else learn, take a marble out of the bowl and put it in the Bank."

James demonstrates and says: "Then name the learning discipline you saw in action, go to the Post-it on the easel, and make a check by that discipline."

He picks up one of the colored markers, reads down the list, makes a check next to "Listens to me," and says: "You were listening to me and that helped a lot."

"If the discipline you saw is not on the list, add it.

"If there is no room on the Post-it, stick it on the wall, and start a new Post-it.

"We will review and update our lists at the end of every week as we evaluate our week together."

(Summary)
"We now have a fool-proof system for making sure that we work in a learning organization. This way we'll learn a lot and have fun, too. Presto. We just created a learning organization."

(Learning Disciplines within a Discipline System)
Starting off the year like this may not eliminate the need for a "discipline system" at first. There will be people in the organization who are so habituated to awards and punishments as motivational tools that it may take some time for them to get back in touch with their internal motivation to learn, regain their drive to create, and relearn how rewarding it is to do things for others.

Furthermore, making learning skills explicit never eliminates the need for boundaries and consequences. "Being kind no matter what" is a requirement for membership in a learning organization, and therefore, of course, "Never be mean" is a rigid law, and appropriate consequences apply.

However, by focusing the students on educational objectives rather than rules, James has made himself the leader of a group of motivated learners. Now his job is helping them with their mission, rather than keeping them in line. Furthermore, defining a social "situation" as a problem-solving opportunity focuses energy where it ought to be—becoming smarter.

Focusing children's attention on a "discipline system" is a waste of human resources, because all children start off loving to love, create, and learn. Teaching them the disciplines of becoming disciplined learners who make valuable contributions to others are welcomed.

Sometimes It's Just That Simple

Kathy Winkler taught a class of twenty-four first and second graders. On the first day of school she gathered them in a circle on the floor of her classroom and said: "In this class we have one rule: Be Kind." In all her years of teaching, she never saw evidence that she needed any other rules.

Furthermore, not only was her classroom characterized by kindness; it was also a fabulous learning environment where it felt like all the students were intensely engaged in mastering their academic skills. Why? All the psychic energy that usually goes into wondering and worrying about social relationships could go into learning reading, writing, mathematics, and sophisticating the social skills required to actually *be* kind.

If you catch kids early enough, it can be just that simple. If a whole school is doing this, and teachers of the older kids are building on the work of the earlier grades, an entire school can be nearly bully free—everyone focusing on what they came here for, to get socially, cognitively and emotionally smarter.

Also, it was completely unnecessary for her to define kindness. All her six to eight-year-olds knew what kindness looked and felt like and what unkindness looked and felt like. No lesson on kindness was necessary, only follow-through and the kind, firm exercise of adult authority.

Of course, there were mistakes. There were teachable moments when children were unkind (knowing kindness and practicing it are two different things). But she had created the context that empowered everyone in the class to move in the kindness direction.

CHAPTER 8

A Leadership Culture Is Obvious to All

Good management is the art of making problems so interesting and their solutions so constructive that everyone wants to get to work and deal with them.

—Paul Hawken

When everyone's genius is engaged it is obvious to all. What is obvious is enthusiasm.

One Thursday morning, I sat in my car in a parking lot facing a nondescript brick building in St. Louis, Missouri. The two-story wall with a double door said "school," even without "The College School" written in big letters twenty feet above me. As I got out of my car and moved toward the door, it opened and a stream of third graders began pouring out, clearly on a mission and entirely engrossed in each other.

When I reached the door and held it open for them, one said, "Thank you." The next said, "Hi!" with a big smile. Nervous, that I had forgotten the name of the principal I summoned up my courage, and when the last student said, "Wait, I forgot my notebook," I bent down and asked her buddy in a fake whisper, "What's the name of the principal?" He looked at me as if to say, "That's random," and said instead, "Sheila."

When I replied, "Thank you," he added, as if not wanting me to get myself in trouble, "She's the Head of the School."

"Oh," I said. "Thank you."

Inside, the school glowed. As I walked down the hallway to the office glancing into the rooms, every child was on a mission. By the time I reached the open door of the office I was beaming from ear to ear, and my heart was floating somewhere just below my chin.

Joyce, the administrative assistant, greeted me warmly and took me into the hallway to show me the full array of student creations on the walls, while we waited for Sheila. Joyce was calmly articulate about the relationships among meaningful content, creative expression, and clear student writing.

In ten minutes, Sheila was greeting me happily and showing me the school. By the time I walked into my first classroom, I had already seen dozens of examples of internally motivated learning. By the time she suggested I get on the bus to go on a field trip I couldn't say no.

I watched sixth graders lead the seventh grade in an environmental education experience, and when there was a lull in the activity I asked a seventh-grade boy, "Do you get a lot of homework?"

"Yes," he said.

Then I asked, "Do you like it?"

"Usually," he replied.

What? Seventh graders liking homework? Well given everything else I had seen I wasn't surprised. When kids are on a mission, they own the work, and the quality of this work showed in every part of The College School.

If our goal is academic achievement, what is our aim?

In her *New York Times* piece "Playing to Learn," Susan Engel writes:

> educators should remember a basic precept of modern developmental science: developmental precursors don't always resemble the skill to which they are leading. For example, saying the alphabet does not particularly help children learn to read. But having extended and complex conversations during toddlerhood does. Simply put, what children need to do in elementary school is not to cram for high school or college, but to develop ways of thinking and behaving that will lead to valuable knowledge and skills later on.

Kids want to learn, and they want to learn what they need to learn to succeed in the world. They know that that includes reading, writing, and all those other academic skills, but they also know that their success depends on a lot more than that.

To be good at mathematics, for instance, a child needs to spend hours practicing arithmetic problems, but she also needs to spend hours drawing pictures, building with blocks, arguing with friends, building playhouses, playing music, or just plain playing on the dance floor, on the playing field, and in the garden.

Instead of aiming high, all too often adults shoot directly at the target and the arrow falls short. Even if all we want for our children is academic success, our aim should be the whole brain. *Treat children the way you would most fondly hope they would be, rather than the novices they seem to be.*

Beth Campbell, a great kindergarten teacher, once said to me: "I see every unused ability in my class as an incipient behavior problem." Well, many schools are awash in unused abilities. We humans are designed to make friends, investigate our environment, make and test hypotheses that might lead to creating useful things and functional relationships. No wonder so many schools don't educate.

In *The Scientist in the Crib: What Early Learning Tells Us about the Mind*, Alison Gopnik shows that babies are scientists. The first five years of life are spent doing experiments to construct a causal map of the world in their brain. Their primary field of study is people. By eighteen months, they can put themselves in someone else's shoes and give them what they seem to want (Harper Collins, 2001).[1]

Children come to kindergarten ready, willing and able to collaborate, create, contribute, figure things out, and grow their interpersonal repertoire; they have been working these problems for forty-three-thousand hours. Yes, of course, we humans are wired for self-defense, but we are also wired to love, to be valuable, and even to devote ourselves to higher purposes. These are core human abilities; failure to utilize them leads to all sorts of behavior problems and other undesirable outcomes up to and including depression, suicide, murder and tyranny, as well as disappointing test scores.

Do our schools use these abilities, or do they say: work on your own, follow directions, guess what's in the teacher's head? Are research, writing, mathematics, and arguing creative activities, or will asking a question put me at risk for ridicule? Is being wrong an opportunity, or should I pretend I'm always right? Do my teachers know that I want to make a difference in the world, or do they only care about how fast I read?

"Look you guys, there are millions of objects and thousands of processes I have to understand. I need your help. You can teach me short-cuts and boundaries so that I don't have to learn the hard way. You can give me work that is more interesting than I could choose for myself. That's great, but there is no substitute for my experimental method. It is my job to figure things out. You see, if I don't engage in the scientific method now, it will be hard for me to learn it later. And how will I build a brain that others can rely on if I only rely on what authority people say?

"I certainly want us to enjoy our time together; so go ahead and say 'No,' or suggest a different activity, or show me how, but don't get mad at me for testing. It's my job. I appreciate anything that helps me build my brain into an organ that will stand the test of perpetual newness." All adults working with children would do well to act as if they have been told this by a child one-hundred times.

CHAPTER 9

Real Authority Brings out the Authority in Others

When the best leader's work is done the people say, "We did it ourselves!"
—Lao Tse

Great teachers are leaders, not managers. When interviewing a teacher don't ask about "classroom management." Engage in conversation that will surface this person's genius. A manager controls variables to achieve predetermined outcomes, a leader creates the conditions for a person's character to show up. Management kills learning; leadership maximizes learning—and (pssst) the test scores go up, too. Educators create the conditions for others to shine, learn, grow, and lead. Management is antithetical to education.

Joan's room was a beehive of active learning all day long. There was no doubt in anyone's mind that each child was being optimally challenged.

Joan taught a mixed group of eighteen first and second graders on her own. A matrix of brass hooks—seven across and eighteen down—screwed to plywood Joan had painted white stood at the entrance of the room. On each hook was a 2 × 4 inch card, white on one side and gold on the other. The left-hand column was gold tags with the names of the eighteen students. Opposite each name hung white cards with a word, symbol, or sticker that indicated an activity. The curriculum was arrayed around the room in dozens of centers of all kinds. Where the material involved progressive degrees of difficulty it was color-coded.

Each day when the students came into the room, the first thing they would do was go to the hook chart, notice what cards Joan had hung up for them, pick one, go to that center, and get to work. Laura, for instance, might have a robin, a rose, a red car, a yellow kite, "math game," and "read to me." Richard might have a blue bird, a tulip, a green truck, and a blue balloon, "math game," and "write a story." Depending on the activity, they might get the work checked by Joan, and when they were finished with an activity, they would go to the hook chart, turn the card over to gold, and pick their next activity.

Joan presented the entire lower elementary school curriculum to all the students, and the upper end was limitless. The structure had infinite flexibility built in. Some kids were mastering multiplication, while others were just starting out. One second grader was reading Shakespeare. One girl was so distractible that Joan gave her one card at a time. A boy with an IQ of 80 spent three years in the room. The Hook Chart said: "Do this. Do that," but the students felt ownership and agency. All members of this very diverse class loved to go to school.

Joan's method was great but not the only way. I have known hundreds of great teachers who all found their own way of teaching so that the students felt they were in charge of their own learning with no compromising on standards. We didn't even think about standards, because the standards were obvious in the activities. We thought about agency.

TREAT THEM AS IF THEY EACH HAVE A TEACHER WITHIN

Years of exposure to this kind of teaching drew me to the original meaning of the word "genius": something each of us has rather than something a few of us are. How to teach all those learning styles? How to make diversity work? How to keep kids from cheating? Bullying? Dropping out? How to prepare citizens for democracy and leadership in a complex, changing world? How to get them to love to go to school every day? Treat them as if they each have a teacher within.

For an educator the curriculum is not an end in itself, but a vehicle for children to build their brains as they create their characters. We create our characters as we take on challenges. Educators lead each character to contribute creatively, effectively, and gracefully to the world. Education is not something we can do to children. Educators can, however, contribute by creating three key conditions (1) high internal motivation (2) high decision making, and (3) high-quality (accurate) feedback. Joan shows us one way of doing it.

At the heart of all this is the art of "High responsibility; Low control." When a person takes responsibility for something it seems intuitively obvious that she needs to have control. How can you have responsibility without control? But that is exactly the question that every parent and teacher needs to answer for herself. All kindergarten teachers worth their salt have it figured out. They know. Bottom line: the kids have to be the actors, the agents, the doers. Education can only occur when a student takes responsibility.

Joan used to say: "My test for myself is: If I leave the room, will the kids keep working as hard as if I were there?" The concept is not new. President Eisenhower said, "Leadership is the art of getting someone else to do something you want done because he wants to do it." Lao-tzu said, "When the best leader's work is done the people say, 'We did it ourselves!'" in the sixth-century BC.

This kind of teaching was revolutionary. That it doesn't sweep the country continues to confound. In 1991 Martin Haberman, a professor at University of Wisconsin, published "The Pedagogy of Poverty Versus Good Teaching" in the December issue of *Phi Delta Kappan*, in which he nicely articulated the damage done by a misuse of authority in a school.

> The classroom atmosphere created by constant teacher direction and student compliance seethes with passive resentment that sometimes bubbles up into overt resistance. Teachers burn out because of the emotional and physical energy that they must expend to maintain their authority every hour of every day. The pedagogy of poverty requires that teachers who begin their careers intending to be helpers, models, guides, stimulators, and caring sources of encouragement transform themselves into directive authoritarians in order to function.[1]

Poverty of the soul and poverty of learning are mutually reinforcing. Perhaps they are the same thing.

CHAPTER 10

~

Don't Teach Empathy. Teach Thoughtfulness

Whosoever shall not receive the kingdom of God as a little child, he shall not enter therein.

—Mark 10:15

So much of what we read about combatting bullying, instilling morality, and teaching empathy leaves out our greatest resource: the natural inclinations of children.

Hannah, Franklyn, and Connor, ages eighteen, twenty, and forty-eight months, respectively, are playing on the other side of a floor-to-ceiling plate glass wall in a small playroom equipped with a climbing structure in the parish hall of a church.

After a good half-hour of playing on their own—climbing stairs, looking out windows, sliding down slides, running clockwise around the structure, running counter-clockwise around the structure, ducking into nooks, squeezing through crannies, and pulling their little bodies up by their hands, Connor decides he needs a check-in with Martha the baby-sitter, who was sitting at a café table ten feet from the door watching all this and sipping coffee.

The door separating them was enormous, massive, and requires all his effort. Undaunted, however, Connor pushes against it and succeeds in squeezing through. Connor covers the ten feet to Martha in no time, but three feet from her chair, Martha jumps up and rushes to the door because Connor's little brother Franklyn, who follows Connor everywhere, is caught. The door has shut on him just as he was halfway through.

No tears, everything fine, and now the two brothers are standing by Martha with one hand on each knee. Suddenly, Connor makes for the door. He has noticed Hannah pushing on the door to get out. Martha is wise enough to let Connor be the rescuer this time. She matter-of-factly says, "Good job, Connor."

Watching Connor at age four one might say—in common parlance—that Connor has been "taught empathy."

If you talk to Martha, however, you discover that it's not that way. It is truer to say that Connor has learned many useful expressions for his natural empathy thus far in the course of his four years of life. Martha claims to have done no more or less than counting on him to want to be helpful, giving him a chance, and recognizing it.

Connor has been one of Martha's babies ever since she began baby-sitting three years ago. Here's another example:

After fifteen minutes of playing in the playroom, all three are out the door again wanting a drink. Two sippy cups stand on the table, and Franklyn takes the blue one. As he brings it up to his lips and turns away from the table, he sees Hannah. Turning back to the table, he picks up the pink cup and gives it to her. The two walk away from the table together sipping. Martha doesn't even bother to comment on this remarkable act of thoughtfulness.

Children learn so much on their own. Most of what they need to learn—from riding a bike to writing—is best taught by coaching them in the act. However, when it comes to learning the most important skill set of life—getting along with others—we often decide to get didactic and ignore internal motivation.

This might even make some sense if adults were such experts at interpersonal conflict—but there isn't much evidence of that. Why do we presume to "teach children right from wrong," when we, ourselves have so much to learn on the subject?

Children are not wired to be selfish—they are actually wired so that by the age of eighteen months they are beginning to take another's point of view and recognize it as different from their own. Children map the social world onto their brain just as they map their linguistic world.

If the name of the game in their world during their first five years is about taking care of each other, and if kindness and cooperation are the norm in their first seven years of school, then their continuing education in the field of "social responsibility" will generally progress quite nicely. If, however, kids have been trying to negotiate unsafe or uncertain environments in their early years, adult lessons about social responsibility will have a hard time sticking.

Ever play give-and-take with babies? They pick a carrot off the tray of their highchair and hold it out to you. You take it, say "Thank you," and give it back to them, but it rarely stops there. They almost always give it back to you. They get more delight at getting the "Thank you," than getting the piece of food.

A four-year-old saving his little brother from a heavy glass door, a two-year-old giving his thirsty little sister his sippy-cup, a fifteen-month-old getting her thirty-month-old big brother to stop raging when the adults were powerless to make him stop, knowing when to give someone else a hug. These are all stories about what it means to be human.

So what can we learn from Martha? Three things are obvious.

1) Don't try to "teach empathy." See children as social animals internally motivated to take on the lifelong challenge of harmonizing the needs of self with the needs of others. See yourself as coach, helping them learn the disciplines of playing the game of life, just as you might teach them how to play soccer.
2) Assume that kids like to do things for others. Act as if making a difference to others is one of the greatest natural joys a human can have and give them opportunities to do it. Let them help. In schools, don't make "community service" something we do to teach altruism once a week, assuaging our conscience so we can get back to our normally selfish behavior the rest of the time. Ask yourself, how many times a day are children given a chance to do something for someone else?
3) Don't avoid conflict. Conflict is woven into the fabric of life, and getting good at it is one of the secrets of a happy life. The more conflicts children get into, the more opportunities you will have to help them learn the disciplines of diplomacy. Notice and name successes; help them analyze failures.

Left to their own instincts and with little positive feedback, an eighteen-month-old might very well get down from the kitchen table, go to the counter to get the milk carton, bring it back, and give it to his big sister, if this is what other people do. Of course, if there are servants, and the family is supposed to sit at the table and be waited on, that behavior is unlikely to occur.

Children are at least 50 percent copycats. They watch carefully to see how things are done around here and create maps in their heads about how they can shape the world so they will be happy in it.

Humans need to be of value to each other. To make our abilities valuable to others is a basic need at least as essential as food, and more essential than security. We even risk our lives for other people. Until psychologists, parents, and other educators get this, we will continue to flounder powerlessly in a sea of narcissism and depression. Want to get dopamine flowing? Make someone else happy.

Beth Campbell's "I see every unused ability in my class as an incipient behavior problem," included her understanding that the natural empathy in children to be her greatest resource. It's a diagnostic tool. Got a problem? Who's got unused abilities?

My third-grade teacher used to make sure that each of us had a job, a way that we should contribute every day to the welfare of the class. Some teachers have kids teach each other. At some schools, every child has a teaching buddy in another class. Students consistently name this as the best thing going on at school. A day when they taught their buddy was a great day no matter what else happened.

As principal, when I needed all the chairs set up in the multipurpose room for an evening event, I didn't ask the maintenance man. I went out to the playground at recess, approached a small knot of third-graders and asked them if they would help me set up the chairs. Only once in thirty-four years did I get a less-than-100 percent enthusiastic reaction. Often other kids would ask me if they could help, too.

Everyone thinks of seventh and eighth graders as especially self-centered, and indeed, middle school is prime time for self-consciousness, self-examination, and self-definition. But in our society, we confuse self-centeredness with selfishness.

More than anything else thirteen-year-olds want to show they are capable of taking on adult responsibility. At St. Paul's eighth graders have kindergarten buddies and at Children's Day School they have preschool buddies. In later years, when they talk about how much they loved their school, they always mentioned their buddy as the best memory of all.

Q: Who are the best baby-sitters? A: Seventh and eighth graders.

Don't underestimate the work that a three-year-old can do. They can learn how to make cupcakes, fold laundry, get the mail, set the table, rake leaves. Dozens of things. Marianne Dunlap of Prairie Flower Montessori School in Decatur can give you a list of about two-hundred examples for all ages.

If you see your child as needing to find ways to participate as a full-fledged member of the body politic, activities will become obvious to you, too. People don't tend to love "chores," but most people like to be on a mission for the people they love. A sign that you are doing something wrong is if you give extrinsic rewards for the work. Paying kids to help around the house is a very bad practice.

If the parental attitude is right, you are doing children a favor when you show them how to do something useful. "How Kids Benefit from Chores" (Wired Magazine, June 2012 by Laura Grace Weldon) has the right idea. It takes for granted that children want to help. What if the basic assumption of the family was that everyone contributed to the welfare of the family?

"Hey, will you help me do the dishes? I'll wash and you dry." If the parent doesn't get an enthusiastic response they are doing something wrong: perhaps timing, tone of voice, or attitude.

As early as one-year-old, many kids love pushing the broom or the mop or the vacuum around. To adults they are pretending to clean, to them, they are preparing to be full-fledged members of the community that is the family. Picking up and organizing toys doesn't need to be a chore if it is something that kids see that everyone does all the time after they are finished using something. They are also developing their body and mind in ways it needs to develop: fine motor skills, gross motor skills, and so on. The trick for a parent is to make small compromises with the requirements of "a job well done," and letting go of the need to get the job done in the "appropriate" amount of time.

Commenting on a blog post about children's natural inclination to be socially responsible, Mary Anderson, principal of a public school in Decatur, Illinois, commented: "Now you've done it. You are giving away all my secrets. All humans have the need to feel important and a part of something bigger than themselves. Children especially feel this need deeply. No greater joy is there than when they are put to a useful task. We must allow people of all ages to show us their best selves and to do that, we must let them help and serve others."

When school people have this same understanding and act on it, a formerly boring school can spring to life. A buddy program, for instance, is where two classes pair up so that older and younger students are learning together. Second graders read to kindergartners once a week. Seventh graders teach fourth graders mathematics. Fifth graders and second graders always have a research project they are collaborating on. In every class, at least once a week the academic skills are taught in the context of a project that involves the kids in making a difference outside the classroom.

Kids who engage in such projects once a week not only have improved test scores but are also more enthusiastic about learning, better able to work with others, and feel more self-confident. Schools that have instituted school-wide buddy projects also have a low incidence of bullying.

A good service-learning project can have the same powerful impact on students' feelings about themselves, their worthiness, their empathy, their problem-solving skills, their academic performance, their sense that they matter. Whenever a school has established such a program from kindergarten through eighth grade, children experience that they matter year after year.

That alone can make schooling an education for each and every student, regardless of widely divergent academic abilities. When a family or community that struggles with basic needs has a strong culture of looking out for and making valuable contributions to the family, the family thrives. A culture of taking care of each other beats a culture of "each man for himself" every time.

MOST PEOPLE LIKE TO BE ON A MISSION FOR PEOPLE THEY LOVE, AND THE MISSION STARTS AT EIGHTEEN MONTHS.

The infinite challenge of harmonizing your needs, values, and interests with those of others is the central challenge for us humans. Looking for opportunities to mobilize the drive to matter, acting as if that other person is more interested in mattering to you than in beating you out is at the core of turning potential conflict into collaborations.

People work for others, they live for others, and they will even die for others. Seeing a school through kids eyes it becomes obvious. *Hmm, Let's see. Should school be doing a bunch of chores, or is school the place I go to lead, love, learn and laugh? So hard for me to decide.* Schools that understand this create cultures where everyone understands that social challenges are the primary vehicle for cognitive development.

If we don't see the empathy in action the way we would like to, it's because either it hasn't been educated, or we aren't looking in the right direction, or both.

"Hey, would you help me . . ."

Say this to children, and you will usually get an enthusiastic, "Sure."

If you get a negative reaction, we can think of several possible causes off the top of our heads:

- It feels imposed rather than offered as an opportunity.
- You think I'm selfish.
- You know it's a job I hate, so you are actually taking advantage of me.
- I feel singled out, . . . and not for greatness.
- I need a little seducing.
- You caught me at a bad time; so you might consider saying something like, "Would there be a better time for you?" (Next time you will be more sensitive to the mission I'm on.)

- You just gave me a lecture on social obligations: "You kids! All you ever want is rights. You have to learn that for every right there is a responsibility." So, obviously, your request is not really in the free-will department but more in the obedience department.

Daily in the blogosphere we read that parents should teach children empathy. No, we shouldn't. We should make sure that our homes and schools are workshops for putting empathy into action, laboratories for learning the uses and misuses of empathy. Rather than trying to "teach" children empathy, we would do better to act as if we know they are already wired for it, see our homes are hotbeds of empathy, and give them opportunities to put their empathy into action—like, say, asking them for help.

In that context, there will be teachable moments, of course—our chance to teach some social skills and do some coaching in emotional control. Under the right circumstances, children actually welcome coaching that will improve their repertoire of skills for harmonizing self and other. Scolding backfires because they are internally motivated to know how to do it on their own.

When a small child investigates an object, one of the moves he always makes is to hold it out to the adult. This is our chance to play the game of give and take. Take it. Say "Thank you, for the spoon," and give it back. When they can talk, they will say "Thank you," too.

Children's brains are designed to know how others feel. They are wired with mirror neurons; when someone else is hurt, they feel it. We also know that children rise (or fall) to our expectations of them. It would be smart to assume they care about others and are working on the never-ending task of understanding other points of view.

Larry Arnstein likes to tell this story about one of his most important experiences as a young child: "One memory I have of play. I was four years old and was supposed to build something with a classmate. I didn't know anybody, so I was scared by this assignment. But there was another child who didn't know anybody, and so we were thrown together. What we were supposed to be doing was making some great structure out of blocks. Neither of us had a clue about what to do. But we knew we were supposed to do something, so we put together a little house we made out of blocks, and we put a sign on it. Our sign was 'Sweet House.' We imagined that our little house would be a place where you could go and buy sweets. I think that our efforts were not rewarded by the teachers, but by that time we didn't care. We were friends. We have remained friends until today."

Larry's is a paradigmatic story about the challenges that all kids face, how they are up to the task, and how they handle those challenges.

Our culture gets in the way here. So steeped are we in seeing the individual as self-determining, self-serving, and self-maximizing, that we tend to see children as selfish. But children know what many adults in our culture often forget: the happiness of others is inextricably connected to our own.

By the time children walk in the door of a kindergarten classroom they have been practicing the art of harmonizing their own needs, wants, and interests with those of others for five years. Talk about an ability! When teachers count on it, their students were always doing things for them, doing things for others, serving the community. A visitor can feel it when they walk in the room.

Adults think they are sending children to school (as if to a sweat shop) to learn the three R's and to climb the ladder of success. Children want to go to school to be with other children, to make friends, to learn more about what they are capable of, and also just to learn stuff. When we honor the genius in children, we find there is plenty of room for a meeting of these two minds.

Children have empathy. Educators know that empathy is one of their greatest abilities, and the origin of some of their greatest passions. The best way to educate it is to utilize it. Acting as if children are naturally selfish is a self-fulfilling enterprise.

CHAPTER 11

A Culture with the Soul of Creativity

The secret of genius is to carry the spirit of the child into old age, which means never losing your enthusiasm.

—Aldous Huxley

Weak, Worried, and Worthless: Myths of the Pyramid Model of Education and Their Antidotes

On the first day of school Leila's mother told her friend Hope: "Leila was looking forward to school all summer. Then two nights ago she started getting anxious."

Knowing that Leila "struggles" with "giftedness," Hope asked, "What was she anxious about?"

"Will my friends be in my classroom this year?"

All children are completely different, each with their own peculiar set of strengths, weaknesses, and things to worry about. However, the number one reason children go to school is to be with other children. Whether they charge into school on the first day all smiles or cling to their parents' legs, they are all the same in one major respect: their highest priority is to avoid embarrassment.

Furthermore, they all know that embarrassment is a possibility for each one of them. "Will I say something stupid in opening circle?" "Will I measure up?" "Will anyone like me?" "Am I worthy?"

We humans are social animals. We all want to be worthy and are aware that our weaknesses put us at risk. We are anxious that our vulnerabilities will trip us up, make us fail or look bad. So in most social environments, we lead with our strengths, trying to hide our weaknesses. In school, life is a race to the top of some pyramid. A few will rise to the top, and the rest . . . well, it's obvious.

In most schools, a great deal of psychic energy goes into trying to hide those weaknesses. The curriculum seems determined to confront me with what I can't do. Some teachers focus on my weaknesses. Others try to pretend they don't exist or focus on my strengths, which only makes me more anxious about my weaknesses. Moreover, my classmates seem committed to expose anything I am trying to hide.

Under these conditions you'd think that those who make it to the top by excelling at the few things schools value: getting good grades, athletic prowess, or popularity would come out unscathed. But even those who have mastered the art of hiding their weaknesses come out haunted by those weaknesses and, therefore, more scathed than anyone in some ways.

Parents and teachers know what we want. We want schools to graduate young people for the world as it is rather than for the industrial age. We want confident, creative collaborators who can communicate, who can speak up and write, and solve problems on their own and also know when to involve others. We want kids who are not into measuring up but rather into making a difference.

Helen's father had a nice way of summarizing it. He would say: "I visited fifteen different schools. I could tell in five minutes that I wanted this school."

"What's so great?"

"All other schools go like this (his hands formed a pyramid); Helen's school goes like this." (The fingers of his hands spread up and out in all directions like a tree.)

We know what he means. Good schools lead children out into the world to manifest themselves in their own peculiar way according to the dictates of their character. The uniqueness of each child manifests itself like the branches on a tree.

The good news is that the changes we want have already occurred in some schools for some students. Hundreds of schools across the country, both public and private, rich and poor, are leadership communities whose cultures are focused on bringing out the best in each person, building their character and their competence, and growing their authority. They have abandoned the Pyramid Model. For these schools and the people in them the game of school is not the "Get the Right Answers Game" but the "Work with Others to Investigate Interesting Questions that Make a Difference Game." These schools are graduating young people for the future—any future.

A SAFE PLACE TO BE MY OWN IMPERFECT, WEIRD, UNIQUE SELF

To liberate us from the myths of an archaic culture and to prepare young people for the emerging global culture. Four changes would make a huge difference:

1. Eliminate the elements of school culture that smack of measuring up.
2. Make diversity a high value and uniqueness the standard.
3. Make the classroom and school a safe place to be yourself.
4. Reorganize the work so that kids pour all their psychic energy into it.

It is possible to do that. Educators—and there are many to use as models—create environments where everyone comes out with a self-image that is neither positive nor negative, but accurate. When school is a safe place to be my own weak, weird, unique self, I can apply 100 percent of myself to the struggle of learning how to face the world with courage and determination. I come out secure in my own unique version of sustainable successfulness, founded on the eternal imperfection of myself and the world. I end up being great.

What's a parent to do?

1. Redefine "worthiness." A parent's definition of worthiness carries weight. Parents' values are hardwired into children by the age of five and can be reinforced as necessary thereafter. We can establish the expectation that struggle, challenge, mistakes, conflict, and disappointment are normal. We can establish effort, resilience, stick-to-itiveness, courage, and the strength-of-character-to-admit-you-were-wrong-and-change-your-mind as values.
2. We accomplish this more by what is in our hearts and minds than by didactic teaching, so we have to own this definition of worthiness ourselves. Children pick up the truth about our values more by osmosis and watching us than by recording what we say. They can detect when we are trying to teach them something, and it feels weird when we try too hard. Our words become suspect.
3. It might be good to say something like: "You know, the best World Series baseball players bat around three-hundred; that means that even the best major leaguers get on base less than a third of the time, and they strike out a lot." (I am sure you can invent better age-and-culturally-appropriate sayings of your own.)

4. Use the words "great" to react to some achievement, something wonderful, Don't use the word "excellent." (Excellent implies comparison with something worse.)
5. Believe in reality:
a. Children are hardwired for struggle, and
b. Struggle, mistakes, loneliness, and conflict are reality.
c. Peace, harmony, success, and winning are artificial constructs of our brains.
6. Support children with empathy. Being empathetic of a child's natural tendency to rise to challenge is essential for strengthening their ability to do it; often it is sufficient. Say, "I know," when they tell you how hard it is.
7. Find allies within the school. Leila's teacher might be thrilled to have a parent who is not on an achievement tear, but a partner in helping her strengthen Leila's disappointment muscle. What if Leila heard, "School is supposed to be hard. What would be the point of sending you to a place that didn't challenge you, . . . and, actually, I believe in you," both at home *and* at school?
8. Parents and teachers can rename the game of school from "Maximize Being Right; Hide Being Wrong," to "Face up to Challenge and Learn."
9. Changing your mind is something you can be proud of.

A Culture with the Soul of Creativity

Ever thought about the fact that four-year-olds know the past tense of ten-thousand verbs having heard only one-hundred or so? You notice this gift when you hear them make a mistake like "goed" or "eated." Equally impressive is how quickly they learn that they are wrong. In no time they are saying "went" and "ate." They handle being wrong better than we adults do.

As Kathryn Shultz so eloquently and entertainingly portrays in *Being Wrong* (HarperCollins, 2010), the human brain has a design flaw: we are brilliant at knowing, equally prone to being wrong and even better at denial.[1]

There are two kinds of learning. "Single loop learning" is adding information to our existing mindsets. "Double loop learning"[2] is changing those mindsets based on new information. This second kind of learning grows out of living in the tension of irreconcilable mindsets to come up with something new. Increasingly, the success of a person, group, or organization depends on our facility with "double loop learning."

Children are better at this than adults, because we adults are under pressure for our mindsets to be accurate and our theories to be true. We think our survival, success, and popularity depend on being right. Less and less, we like to change our theories, so more and more we're prone to arrogance—often with devastating results.

So, what do we have to do to stop stepping off into wrongness?

1. ask questions
2. talk to a friend
3. sleep on it
4. increase awareness
5. let go of expectations
6. lollygag, meditate, wonder, go for long walks
7. pay attention to crazy ideas
8. play
9. publically own your thoughts and feelings
10. experiment with new behaviors
11. invite disconfirmation
12. ask the person who didn't say anything at the meeting what she thinks before you vote.

These disciplines and many others tend toward inviting our genius to the table. This inner voice of the soul is aware of *all* the data including what we have been avoiding, ignoring, or denying.

Culture is powerful. The culture we are in can either drive us toward needing to be right or open our eyes to wrongness and new possibilities. In most schools, for instance, these twelve behaviors are too risky, odd, or not allowed. Being wrong is embarrassing because only being right is valued. Asking stupid questions or changing your mind might get you laughed at. Talking to a friend or lollygagging might get you yelled at.

On the other hand, we can actually create culture by defining ourselves to the situation moment by moment. We can look for opportunities to speak the truth in ways that get smiles instead of snarls. We can be the child who says, "The emperor has no clothes." We might have to risk being weird, but then we might contribute to learning, and more importantly we'll have surfaced more truth for a more creative climate. This is leadership.

Leaders can create a culture where one gets as many brownie points for making mistakes as for being right. Parents can change the culture in the home by acknowledging their mistakes instead of hiding them. Removing the recrimination layer from conflict can have a powerful effect on turning conflicts into successful collaborations. Giving children opportunities to take responsibility for others completely obviates the need to lecture them on "being responsible," or to "teach them empathy."

Our genius (and we each have one) is the key to liberating us from our cultural prisons. Genius is expert in harmonizing inconsistent opposites, resolving dilemmas, and integrating of two impossibilities. Reality and our trusted beliefs never quite match up. Our soul holds the key to living with the confusion long enough for us to create something of value.

Living with our paradoxes leads us down into our soul and back out toward creativity.

CHAPTER 12

Conflict Aversion Is a Learning Disability

All the ills of mankind, all the tragic misfortunes that fill the history books, all the political blunders, all the failures of the great leaders have arisen merely from a lack of skill at dancing.

—Molière

Getting to Yes

In 1984, I heard Roger Fisher speak at a conference. At the time Fisher was the Director of the Harvard Negotiation Project, author of the Camp David accords that brought peace to Egypt and Israel in 1978, and author of *Getting to Yes* (1981)[1]. I still I remember his talk. He started with:

"I am in the conflict business. You are in the conflict business."

We all laughed a laugh of recognition, as if with one voice, we all acknowledged that it was true. When you run a school you are clearly in the conflict business.

He ended his talk by holding up a fist and saying: "So if you find your hand clenched in a fist, remember five things": then, opening one finger with each statement, said:

"Separate the person from the problem."
"Get beneath positions to interests."
"Always insist on objective criteria."
"Generate multiple options for mutual satisfaction."
"Always go into a conflict with your Best Alternative to a Negotiated Agreement (BATNA)."

and then, because he had opened one finger for each point, he was able to say:

"And then you will find your hand open and ready to shake hands with your enemy."

Comfort with conflict is at the core of a culture that prepares young people for leading creative, effective, and graceful lives in a democracy. Conflicts are opportunities to define ourselves, build partnerships, and create value. We need practice, and we need leaders who are practiced at making conflict creative. We must act as if this kind of leadership is up to us.

Remove the Recrimination Layer

One Saturday morning, thirty-some years ago, my thirteen-year-old son Peter arrived in the kitchen as I was having my morning coffee. Rather than greeting me with, "Good morning, Dad" he went straight to the refrigerator, took out a carton of orange juice, grabbed a large glass from the cupboard, and filled it to the brim.

"Wow. That's a lot of orange juice," I said. (I don't know why. "Good morning, Peter," certainly would have been a better opener.) Still, I didn't. I said: "Wow, that's a lot of orange juice."

Standing in the middle of the kitchen floor in bare feet with the glass of orange juice in his hand and looking squarely at me, Peter flew into a rage with: "You are always on my case! Why are you always on my case? Nothing I ever do is right!" and went on in that vein for a minute or so.

During a moment of speechless surprise, a smile slowly spread over my face. After a thoughtful pause, I said, "We belong to mutual confrontation society, don't we?"

He laughed. I laughed, and then we both laughed together. From that moment on I was blessed with a hassle-free relationship with my adolescent son. It was like magic.

I am sure we must have had some conflicts after that, but honestly, I don't remember them. My recollection is of a hassle-free adolescence.

What did I do right? I saw that I was in a conflict and embraced it. Embracing the conflict was like embracing my son.

FIVE DISCIPLINES OF DEFINING YOUR SELF TO A CONFLICT TO INCREASE THE LIKELIHOOD THAT IT WILL BE A COLLABORATION

1. Treat the other person the way you most fondly hope they would be, rather than the _____ they are proving themselves to be. "That person is not the problem."
2. Treat people the way THEY want to be treated. Look beneath behavior and positions to interests, needs, values, and genius.
3. Be specific. Say it so it plays like a movie in our heads.
4. Collaborate creatively on multiple options for mutual satisfaction.
5. Find your point of integrity so if that other person IS a jerk, you will be prepared with your best unilateral move. (You might want to start here.)

These five disciplines of turning a conflict into a collaboration are well known by those who know they are in the conflict business: diplomats, politicians, and salesmen.

With Peter, all I needed was the first one: "Yes, we have a problem here, but you are not the problem." When conflict is in the air, it usually exists on two levels: the conflict itself and "the recrimination layer"—the notion that we shouldn't even be having this conflict, at all. When I said, "We belong to a mutual confrontation society, don't we?" I removed the recrimination layer and communicated, "You are not the problem."

"BEST PRACTICES" ARE NOT AROUND IN A MOMENT OF CRISIS—OUR GENIUS IS.

"We belong to mutual confrontation society, don't we?" Those words. Where did they come from? They did not come from a parenting book. They just popped out of me. Whatever we learn from parenting books, lists of good practices, "Rules for Fair Fighting," and so on, are not available to us in at a moment of crisis—our genius is.

Self-control, perspective taking, connecting, communicating, collaborating, creating, and changing our minds—these are the skill sets we all need. Taking stands, making the difference we need to make, becoming the characters we are meant to become, is our real work and conflict is where a great deal of this brain development happens. To make these conflicts creative, we must listen to the voice of our soul.

Chapter 12

How to Handle a Bad Teacher

You must do the things you think you cannot do.

—Eleanor Roosevelt

At dinner one evening twenty years ago shortly after the start of her sophomore year in high school, my daughter, Lizzie, said, "The new science teacher is not a good teacher. He just isn't teaching right. I can't understand what he's trying to do."

I said, "Well, you have to go talk to him, I guess."

"I couldn't do that."

"Why can't you?"

"I just can't."

"Well, then talk to the Principal."

"No, I would never do that!"

"Well . . ."

"Dad! I don't want to talk about it!"

The next night at dinner she said, "I talked to the Dean."

"Great. What happened?"

"I can tell that she talked to him, because he changed, but what he did was worse. Now, I'm even more frustrated."

"Well," I said. "Now you *have* to go back to the Dean and give her feedback on the results."

"I can't do that." She said.

"Yes you can. It's only . . ."

"Dad, I don't want to talk about it."

The next night she reported, again: "I did talk to the Dean, again, and she obviously talked to *him* again, because he changed even more, . . . but it got even worse."

"Wow. That's interesting."

"But, you know what I learned?" she said. "I learned how I can learn from him."

I was happy that she thought she would be learning some science this year, but I was thrilled that she had shown that she was making good progress in the skills of success in life.

Look at the skills Lizzie was practicing by taking on this challenge:

1. Turning a frustration into a problem to be solved,
2. Identifying a conflict,
3. Verbalizing the conflict in a way understandable to someone else,
4. Enlisting someone's help with the problem,
5. Making a plan,
6. Taking action,
7. Observing the results,
8. Adjusting her thinking,
9. Making a new plan,
10. Implementing the new plan,
11. Learning from the results,
12. Redefining the problem,

Most importantly, she changed herself so that she could continue her education under new conditions. Exercising these mental capacities develops not just Lizzie's executive self (centered in her prefrontal cortex) but also her ability to find resources inside herself, resources she didn't know she had, resources that continue to help her lead a life of continuous leading, learning, and loving.

In Lizzie's experience with the bad science teacher, what did Lizzie do right?

First, she told me to keep out of it. She seemed to know that taking on this conflict was something she had to do herself (internally motivated decision-making). Then, trusting in something inside her, she formed a partnership with someone who had a reasonable prospect for helping her: the Dean. She worked the problem by building relationships.

CHAPTER 13

Conflict Is the Crucible of Character

The problems of three little people don't amount to a hill of beans in this crazy world.

—Rick in Casablanca

Conflict Is Social Problem Solving

Three boys appeared in the door of the principal's office.

Boy 1: "We're not in trouble. Our teacher sent us to ask if you could help us work out a problem that came up at recess."

She excused herself from the finance meeting, and the boys gathered around her at a chair in the hallway.

Boy 2: "We got into a fight."

Principal: "Do you think you can work it out yourselves?"

Boy 3: "We want to try to work it out ourselves."

Principal: "Okay. Tell you what. You guys sit at the table in the courtyard outside my window, and if you run into trouble, raise your hands, and I will leave my meeting and help." As they walked outside, the principal said, "Let's move the table closer to the window." Together they moved the table closer to the office window so she could be a presence. Then she went back to her meeting.

After about ten minutes of animated talk a hand went up. One of them came over and said that there was a fourth boy who should be sitting at the table. She said, "Okay, one of you go get him." Soon there were four at the table. After about ten more minutes the principal decided it was time to see how they were doing, so she left the meeting again and pulled a chair up to the head of the table.

They took turns talking, building on each other's ideas, and obviously trying to come to a consensus. They kept changing their minds until they all agreed they had a plan.

"What's your plan?" the principal asked.

"When we find ourselves getting mad at each other, we'll take a break."

"Yeah, we'll just sit down till we cool down."

Principal: "That's good: 'Sit down till you cool down.'"

"Yeah, or kick the ball with our teammate till we are ready to play again."

Principal: "Good job. Let's see how it works. Will one of you take responsibility for coming and reporting to me?"

Boy 4: "I will."

What's so important about this story? (1) The boys took responsibility for their conflict and by taking responsibility worked on their collaborative skills and thus added to their conflict resolution repertoire. (2) The teacher correctly assessed their readiness for working out this conflict on their own, thus creating the space for them to actually learn, develop and practice those skills. (3) The principal was used correctly: as an educator who is available to help people with their learning challenges rather than an officer of the law. No one was "in trouble." No one was "bad." Conflicts are to be expected in a human community, and we might as well welcome them as learning opportunities.

Adults often try to "encourage" children to "be responsible" and get mixed results. This is because the language is tragically flawed. "Being responsible" is a static trait, and to a child's ear the message is "You don't have this trait and you need it." They feel labeled rather than encouraged. Labels (both good and bad) are bad encouragement.

A better focus for children is the requirement: "take responsibility." When we take responsibility for something, we feel good because we are challenging our abilities to respond to a situation with internal motivation. "Ability" is inert and useless without "response." Ability is only real when used in the act of taking responsibility for something—like your work or your relationships.

In a functional learning community respect and responsibility are not "values," but laws. (1) Be respectful at all times no matter what. (2) Take responsibility for your work and your relationships. The principal can be useful as a reminder that this is so. To develop the experience of justice in each of us, each of us has to keep taking responsibility for situations of ever-increasing complexity.

CHAPTER 14

Conflict Is Required for Creating Character

Little girls are cute and small only to adults.
To one another they are not cute. They are life-sized.

~Margaret Atwood

Children under seven don't merely exist. Children live. Of course, they don't "know how to live"; no one really knows that. They just act as if they know that their job is to learn how to live and that the best way for them to learn that is just to go ahead and live, learning as they go, growing that little thing inside them that started as an acorn—their character.

The development of character is not simply doing the right thing nor is it doing your own thing and being "a character." We develop our character in conflict with other characters.

We are wired for cooperation. And, we are wired for competition. Others are a potential threat and others are potential allies. Conflict and cooperation are instinctive with humans. We all want to be valuable in a group and to form productive relationships with others, but it is not easy. Other people—those individuals we want to form partnerships with—have minds of their own—needs, values, interests, and abilities that make forming teams infinitely challenging.

We need other people, but other people are a problem. For best results, we should understand all relationships as conflictual, dive in, and get good at conflict. Only then can we turn potential enemies into friends. The secret ingredient in bringing out leadership in ourselves and in others at the same time is to act as if each of us has a genius and to know that these geniuses are in league with each other.

Besides, working things out with others is great for brain development. In fact, working things out with others was a major driver of human evolution.

And it's still going on, today. One Tuesday afternoon on the playground after rest time, Riley, Sarah, and Anya (all preschoolers) were discussing what to play. They all decided that they wanted to be sisters, but became stuck when they had to figure out who would be what sister. Riley wanted to be the baby sister and both Sarah and Anya wanted to be the medium sister. They both ran up to Ms. Margaret, upset.

"I want to be the medium sister and Anya wants to be the medium sister, too, and I'm really a medium sister!" wailed Sarah, who really had a big sister, Laurel, and a brand-new baby sister, Cecilia.

"But I want to be the medium sister, too, and it's not fair!" exclaimed Anya.

"Well, how could you solve this problem? Maybe you could both be the medium sister?" said the wise teacher channeling King Solomon.

"But we can't both do it! Then there would be nobody to be the big sister and you can't have two medium sisters and no big sister!" cried Sarah. She had a point.

"Yeah! We need a big sister and I want to be the medium sister too!" shouted Anya.

"Well, maybe you need another person in your game, then," said Margaret.

Sarah and Anya both looked around the yard. Both girls' eyes stopped on Meghan who was carefully trying out a new trick, crawling from picnic bench to picnic bench right nearby.

Sarah nudged Anya. "Maybe Meghan wants to be a sister with us?"

"Yeah!" cried Anya.

"Meghan, do you want to play with us?" called Sarah.

"Um, okay! Just let me finish my trick," Meghan said to the two older girls.[1]

Meghan crawled to the end of the bench and jumped off. Sarah grabbed her hand and the three of them ran off to baby sister (Riley). As they were running off, Sarah said, "Come on, Meghan! You get to be the big sister, me and Anya are medium sisters, and Riley's the baby sister."

Nobody likes conflict; and yet, conflict is the engine of learning. Character does not grow like a flower—all you have to do is water it. Character develops in adversity.

Out in the yard when Anya, Riley, Meghan, and Sarah had that character-building moment, something else happened, too. As each was working for herself, empathy caused love to get involved, and justice prevailed. Even though there is no truth to the idea that Riley is the little sister, it was truly a beautiful moment. Besides, whoever thought there could be two "medium sisters"?

The Highest and Best Use of a Cookie

. . . a stage, where every man must play a part

—William Shakespeare

Anya, Riley, Meghan, and Sarah found a win-win solution to their social problem. This is not an unusual or unnatural event—in fact, we adults should expect it. Even before they get to kindergarten, children are masters at finding that point of mutuality between their self-interest and the interests of others. This is especially true for girls.

It is initially puzzling, therefore, that girls become so mean to each other in fourth grade. Educators, who consistently experience this phenomenon, have come to expect it. Nine years old is, after all, a marker for a developmental stage in children (plus or minus a year). It is an age of individuation. Educator and author of *Kingdom of Childhood*, Rudolf Steiner observed:

> When the child reaches his ninth or tenth year he begins to differentiate himself from his environment. For the first time there is a difference between subject and object; subject is what belongs to oneself, object is what belongs to the other person or other thing; and now we can begin to speak of external things as such, whereas before this time we must treat them as though these external objects formed one whole together with the child's own body. (9)

Watching socially skilled fourth-grade girls being mean to each other I think:

Maybe this behavior is more clumsy than mean.

Maybe what happens is that girls reach a level of self-reflection that allows them to see moral dilemmas from a new more self-consciously selfish point of view.

Whereas in the past they may have naturally sensed the wisdom of giving up something for the sake of the relationship, now their reaction to a moral dilemma is to side with themselves over others. By this age they have become so experienced at harmonizing their feelings with the feelings of others, that it is less important to them than individuating. The new challenge of self-definition is so important that they seem willing to put their long-time friendships at risk.

When Thelma was in fourth grade, she added a new line to her very considerable verbal repertoire. She started to begin sentences with "No offense, but . . ."

One day, her teacher, who had been watching her cause offense to others for a week or so, took her aside on the playground and said: "I know you don't want to offend people, right?"

"No. Of course not," said Thelma.

"Well," said her teacher, "To introduce criticism with 'No offense, but . . .' is automatically offensive."

"Why," asked Thelma.

"Using the word 'offense,' alerts the listener that you are in the possibly offensive zone, and so I am expecting to be offended rather than expecting *not* to be offended. It's the same way if I begin a sentence with 'I'll be honest with you . . . .' (It makes me suspicious.) It would work a lot better if you introduced the negative feedback with 'May I talk with you about something that is bothering me?'"

Thelma got it, immediately, and never said it again. Sometimes we just need to given them their lines.

It is, of course, not as simple as this; how kids treat one another has many dimensions. One year the fourth-grade teachers decided to use their study of illegal immigration to get at the social problems in the class. In order to give the students a more personal understanding of some of the issues involved in immigration, three children were identified as "illegal immigrants" for the day.

All the other students were either "citizens" or "lawful permanent residents." Throughout the morning, the illegal immigrants (Asher, Alena, and Erin, randomly chosen out of the "feely box") had to do extra jobs or missed out on fun things like recess. At snack time, the teachers gave out cookies to everyone—except the illegal immigrants. Most of the other kids noticed that this was unfair, but they accepted and ate their cookies anyway.

However, very, very quietly, Leyla snuck up to the illegal immigrants and whispered to them that she wanted to share her cookie with them, even if this meant she would be "sent to jail." One by one, she took them into the cloakroom and gave them her cookie to share.

The beginning of responsible civil disobedience?

Maybe. My guess is that Leyla's empathy kicked in. She felt bad for her classmates—for the indignities and suffering they had to endure as illegal immigrants.

Maybe, she even felt guilty.

Maybe she just wasn't that hungry. The teacher wanted to believe that she stood up to authority in the name of justice.

Maybe someone should ask Leyla why she did it.

KIDS DON'T SO MUCH NEED TO BE TAUGHT EMPATHY AS GIVEN PRACTICE IN DEVELOPING THEIR EMPATHY REPERTOIRE

But whatever her motivation, she experienced the joys of being kind.

And I think we can all agree that if she was being self-centered, she was being smart about it. For the benefits of being kind: friendship, happy community, just the joy of giving—far outweighed the loss of the cookie.

I think we can all agree that she found a higher and better use of her cookie.

"Teach Empathy" has become a popular war-cry these days, but recent research supports what I have noticed from working in schools; that is, that children like being of service (Marilyn Price Mitchel, 2015) and don't so much need to be taught empathy as thoughtfulness (Kuhl 2007, Bloom 2012).[2] We all need to be thoughtful about how to channel our empathy in constructive directions, to increase our repertoire of interpersonal actions and reactions and given practice in developing our empathy repertoire.

Thoughtful. Isn't that what school is supposed to teach? Aren't social challenges great places to develop our thinking skills? Empathy? "If you prick me, do I not bleed?"[3]

These concepts are actually easier for children to get than adults. Kids actually want to make a difference. They know that education includes a lot more than what's on the tests and that being with other kids is the primary reason for going to school.

Working on your problem-solving skills makes you smarter whether you hone them by practicing them on other people (like uncreative teachers) or by struggling to write an essay or solving social problems on the playground. The human brain is naturally designed to take on social challenges, direct energies toward a goal, change perspective, connect, communicate, think critically, and creatively because the organism wants to make something of itself and be valuable.

Education is essentially anti-tyranny training.

Seeing a potential enemy as a friend requires imagination.

Finding an outcome that transcends a disagreement requires imagination.

Thinking of better ways of expressing ourselves requires imagination.

Growing stronger requires imagining a deeper self.

Classrooms that don't reward imagination need redesign because children need lots of practice building leadership skills. Arguing lovingly must be an educational objective built into the culture and practiced every day.

From the sandbox to the classroom to the seminar to the workplace to the boardroom to the Situation Room, collaborating, creating, and contributing is our business. Delivering on this requires redesigning school cultures. Leadership by anyone can move us toward creative cultures. The amount of conflict a leader will be experiencing depends on the degree of functionality of the culture she is in.

CHAPTER 15

Treat Kids As If Social Responsibility Is a Natural Act

Only a life lived for others is worthwhile

—Albert Einstein

Most Americans would expect that if you put two-hundred children in one room for an hour near the end of the school year, there would be some discipline problems. Last week I attended an hour-long assembly where twenty first, second and third graders, performed for one hundred eighty first-through-eighth graders. I detected no discipline problems. No. I guess I did see one teacher beckon for a child to come sit next to her.

This was an end-of-the-year production at Golden Oak Montessori, a public charter school in Hayward, CA. Golden Oak demonstrates the validity of the dictum: treat children as if being socially responsible is something children would naturally want to be. (*"Why wouldn't I? I'm not saying it is always easy. I'm just sayin' it's the thing I care most about."*)

Anywhere you go in the school, children are just being children and being socially responsible at the same time. One eight-year-old came charging around the corner and bumped into me. He stopped, said, "I'm sorry," waited for me to smile back with "that's okay," and we both went on about our business. In the classrooms and out, the children ages seven to fourteen are going about their business of learning—and learning includes (of course) learning how to get along with others.

American culture is biased toward individuality. We expect kids to simply want to "do their own thing." "I gotta be me" is foundational to American economic and political democracy. Emerson's *"Self-Reliance"*[1] is a cornerstone of our society.

But today, self-reliance has lost its way in a sea of self-absorption. We often see people trying to be true to themselves as if they live and move in spiritual isolation. Today, "being yourself" is more about by-passing social hurdles and doing exactly what you want on the way to the inalienable right of happiness.

But if "decision-making" doesn't include good social decision-making, we are often a frustration to others, as well as ourselves. The harder we try to get happy without including those around us, the more we perpetuate our unhappiness. For humans, just as for ants and bees, the basic organism is the colony, the hive, the group, the community, not the "individual."

This self-absorption brings with it a concomitant confusion about community, rules, discipline, social responsibility, and justice. Belief in the sanctity of the individual child translates all too often into acting as if our adult needs, the needs of the community, the needs of others, are unfortunate impositions upon the child.

Parents and teachers say "guidelines" when they mean rules, give kids choices when there really is only one responsible choice, and say, "listen" when they mean "obey." A teacher will say something like, "Julian had a hard day today," when the truth is that *she* had a hard day dealing with Julian. Parents are often stymied by the willfulness of their children. To quote one mother asking for advice: "Ashley is a delightful child but very willful, and I don't want to break her spirit."

We are in constant tension between self and other. But both self and other are inside us, and out of this constant conflict grows something new, something stronger, something often better than the Self we had in mind in the first place.

The development of character is not simply doing the right thing nor is it doing your own thing and being "a character." Rather, character (the self-that-is-becoming) is the result of a dynamic relationship between the self and its environment, a tension that educates both the self and others, a conflict that creates new and often wonderful moments—moments of beauty, truth, love, and justice. Kids actually understand that.

When efforts at "discipline" fail, it is because they are delivered under the false assumption that selfishness is natural and altruism is unnatural.

All day long Golden Oak points to the reality that a human is both a unique individual and a web of relationships striving to become whole. Educators do well to correct children's behavior as if the children know and care about their relationships and fundamentally want to do the right thing.

At 8:26 a.m., one morning out in front of the school, the principal stepped away from her job of shaking hands and greeting incoming students at the front door of the school to talk to a student in the hallway. When she returned to her post one minute later she found Isabel and Isabella, two fifth-graders, standing where she had been standing, shaking hands, smiling and saying good morning to the students as they came into school.

The next day a group of students took this responsibility on as one of their regular responsibilities and now it is a tradition at the school for students to help the head of school open car doors and greet the students. It is no small deal for teens and tweens to choose to take time away from their primary occupation of hanging out with each other and take responsibility for opening car doors and welcoming the students into school.

Another Moment

Ten-year-old Yasmin easily went up a thirty-foot climbing wall and rang the bell at the top. Her partner Violet, however, got halfway up and stopped. It was hard, and she didn't want to push on. But Yasmin, her challenge met, didn't climb back down. Instead, she talked to Violet, encouraging her to keep going. And Violet did. She started climbing again, climbed up to where Yasmin was waiting for her and rang the bell. The two girls came down together.

Yasmin had helped Violet push herself farther than she thought she could go, and Violet didn't give up and felt proud that she had accomplished something she didn't think could.

The adults were impressed that the girl who had made it to the top had helped the other girl to the top. But talking about the event afterward Violet said, "We encouraged each other and brought out the best in each other." Yasmin agreed. "It's all about friendship."

Another Moment

Jasmine and Aymani were sitting together editing each other's papers. Shelby who was sitting nearby overheard them wrestling with the problem of how to indicate to each other the things that needed fixing. She said, "There are signs you can use." By the end of the day a team of half-a-dozen students had collaboratively created two new sets of editing tools: a stack of laminated 3 x 5 cards that would facilitate the communication between students as they helped each other improve their writing, and a game for memorizing the symbols of editing.

Another Moment

Two fifth graders came to the third-grade classroom asked the teachers permission to talk to two boys. Out in the hallway they confronted the boys with the mess they had made with paper towels in the boy's bathroom at recess. The recalcitrants asked their teacher if they could go clean up their mess. She agreed, and they did. The teacher of the accused simply stood in support.

Another Moment

In Ben's Upper Elementary classroom students were engaged in a lively discussion. He had asked them how they felt about helping other people.

"When you help others, you are helping yourself. You get a reward. People will respect your kindness."

"Yes. Your reward could be something you learn along the way. As you help someone else, you can learn things. That's a reward."

"Well, I disagree a little. I don't think you help others for a reward. I think you should help others for the sake of kindness, not rewards."

"Helping others for a reward is not genuine."

"I agree. If everyone thinks of others, you won't need to care about yourself as much. I care about others, but I have to work at showing it. It makes me feel better."

Discussions like this happen on a regular basis in all classrooms from first grade through eighth.

Are children always generous and thoughtful of others? Of course not. In fact, children start making distinctions between those they should love and those they should fear, from birth. They begin to generate and test hypotheses about social relationships and build a causal map in their brains about how the social world works. They want to know (in fact, they know they *need* to know) how they can best manifest themselves in the world. As they do their social research, they try out all sorts of behaviors, everything from giving to taking, from being kind to being mean, from helping to getting in the way. They learn when generosity, reciprocity, or selfishness works by trial and error.

Certainly, children are self-centered. They are developing themselves. But just because they are self-centered doesn't mean they have to be selfish. "Only a life lived for others is a life worthwhile?" Yes, and children already sense the truth of this. Learning that giving is, in fact, more happy-making than receiving is quite natural.

In this school fourth, fifth, and sixth graders are sophisticating their notions of how this is true and how to experience it; of course, they are. They have been sophisticating these notions since they first walked in the doors of this wonderful school.

In one class there is a child with serious, life-threatening allergies. The children take responsibility for keeping him safe without any reminders from a teacher. In middle school, every morning the students lead an organizational meeting in which they take responsibility for building their learning organization. It is a social work of art.

A former colleague tells this story about some of the social animals he was in charge of—and some he was not.

At a Boys and Girls Club in San Francisco over spring vacation Cam and Aiden, two second graders from a private school, were throwing a football around with kindergarteners Deena and Jayden, when four public school ten-year-olds came over and asked if they could play. Dan, the teacher, anxious about what might happen, decided to stay and watch. He thought he would at least have to organize the teams and referee to keep the younger kids safe, but he soon discovered how wrong he was.

Cam quickly organized everyone into teams: private vs. public, and the eight young people launched seriously into a game of touch football with other activities swirling around them in the large gymnasium.

The teacher was concerned that the teams were unfair; the older kids were so much bigger. But again, he was wise enough to wait and see. The younger students quickly realized that Aiden and Deena were too speedy and shifty to be caught, and they began improvising handoffs and reverses executed by quarterback Jayden and directed by Cam. Jayden hardly came up to the waist of the opponents, yet time and again, he was able to throw the ball just over their hands, either Deena or Aiden would race to grab it and take off. The game continued without let-up for an hour and a half.

But what impressed the teacher most was the students' ability to resolve conflicts. They collectively decided how they would handle kicking extra points and agreed that certain markings on the walls would be goalposts. From time to time the game would be halted by a big disagreement about rules or whether someone had been touched or gone out of bounds. Each time, the game stopped until the dispute was resolved.

Several times the teacher thought he would have to mediate, but each time, he discovered that the students, themselves, had matters well in hand. The little ones confidently debated issues with strangers a foot taller than they were, and each time, they all agreed on a resolution or a do-over. Nobody was going to let too much time, get wasted before they could play again.

The game attracted the attention of some other adults who watched the proceedings together for a while. "How is it that are these younger ones are doing so well?" asked one club worker.

"Because they're being a better team!" answered another.

Of course, it was good that the teacher was watching. There are times when children need adult intervention. But why do adults think children won't learn to be kind if we don't teach them? Certainly not because adults are so good at it. A little self-awareness would be appropriate here. In our culture, adults need to bring in lawyers to handle the dirty work of conflict precisely because we hate it and are bad at it.

At their childish level kids can often do better on their own. If children are not doing any better on their own, perhaps they have been watching adults and mirroring back what they see.

We are social beings. Being happy and successful in life requires being thoughtful of others, reading other minds, finding common interests, harmonizing your wants with theirs, and engaging in collective action. *Homo sapiens* would never have gotten this far if we weren't naturally good at cooperation.

At Another School

One beautiful spring day, I walked through the double glass door of a large, brick box of a school building that houses the Baker Demonstration School in Evanston, Illinois. To my right was the Principal's Office, but on my left were two three-year-olds who greeted me with: "Good morning. Would you like to come to our art gallery?"

"Why yes, of course," I replied.

"Admission is five cents," the boy said.

"Rats," I answered. "I don't have any coins."

"That's okay," said the girl. "Here is a bowl of pennies. It's okay if you use them."

"Wonderful. Thank you." I took seven, followed them to a little red cash register on a little wooden desk just inside the door of the classroom, and handed them to the young man, who carefully counted out five pennies, put them in the register, and handed me a little, red "Ticket" and two pennies. "Here's your change," he said.

The girl then took me into the room full of little people (and two big ones) and introduced me to two others with, "This is Amber and Rachel. They will show you around," which they did quite professionally.

What I saw in this pre-school class I saw everywhere as I walked around the school. Everywhere from kindergarten to eighth grade, I saw children of all ages making a difference to others, doing valuable things that had meaning for them, making decisions, obviously comfortable in their own skins, apparently loving learning and taking it for granted. Creativity abounded—evidence was even hanging from the ceiling. It seems nothing is done without creativity, and the academic product is obvious everywhere from the writing and graphs on the walls, to the conversation in the fifth grade. The teachers are teaching, all right, but it looks like the kids are doing all the work.

Baker Demonstration School is not a school for the gifted. Clara Belle Baker founded it in 1918 to demonstrate "how the mind learns," and to graduate children who "love to learn, cherish the journey and serve the world." Its success at doing this is obvious.

What is its secret sauce? The professionals in the school have a lot to say about that, but an outsider can guess that *Treat children as if they know what they are doing* is an assumption built into everything the adults do.

Children are vastly more capable than most schools give them credit for. When schools don't get the kind of results that schools like Baker get, maybe it is because the whole program underestimates children. The culture of Baker assumes that the kinds of skills the world will require of our graduates: focusing, making connections, changing perspective, creating, making judgments, finding meaning, working with others, managing conflict, planning, taking on challenges, persevering, etc., are the very skills that children want to acquire. Of course, why wouldn't they? (Educators from *Tony Wagner at Harvard*[2] to *Linda Darling-Hammond at Stanford*[3] keep reminding us.)

What parents and teachers tend to ignore is that the human organism is naturally designed to do all this. Children naturally want to continue this complex engagement with the world, and many cannot tolerate *not* having these abilities used, developed, sophisticated, and practiced. Humans need this kind of engagement as much as they need sleep and exercise. Social, emotional, and cognitive deprivation is the root cause of low academic achievement, the increased dropout rate and the poor quality of our work force. Most schools are partly to blame for this deprivation.

CHAPTER 16

To Get Results, Schools Must Be in the Friendship Business

Why do we have a brain in the first place? Not to write books, articles, or plays; not to do science or play music. Brains develop because they are an expedient way of managing life in a body.

—Antonio Damasio

Father: "It is so hard to get the kids out of the house in the morning, Karen and Matt keep fighting. This sibling rivalry is driving me crazy, but I don't want them to be late to school."

Advice from the principal: "Put a chair in front of the front door, sit in it with arms folded and consider saying something like this: 'I will not take you to school until you can show me that you are ready to work out your differences and be supportive of each other. If you are this incompetent before you even get to school, how do you expect to be successful in school?'"

That this advice sounds laughably extreme and never practiced proves that our culture is unclear about what it means to be educated.

Ask most teachers, today, about the mission they are on and they will say things like "Give kids twenty-first-century skills," "Prepare young people for an increasingly diverse, complex, changing, challenging world."

SCHOOL: A VARSITY SLEEPOVER LED BY PROFESSIONALS!

Parents, also, are predisposed to such a mission and want their kids not only to be academically prepared but also to be "lifelong learners" who are "good at working with others" and "comfortable in their own skin." Then many teachers and parents go off to school and forget their mission.

Children are born interdependent, and they know it. We miss our biggest opportunities when we see children as caught on the horns of a dilemma between dependence and independence—having to make the choice: am I selfish or selfless? They know, what we all should know, that we have the challenge everyday of harmonizing our needs, values and interests with those of others.

In "Social Animal" (*The New Yorker*, January 17, 2011)[1] David Brooks writes about "How the new sciences of human nature can help make sense of life." He writes: "the traits that do make a difference . . . are 'the ability to understand and inspire people; to read situations and understand the underlying patterns; to build trusting relationships; to recognize and correct one's shortcomings; to imagine alternative futures.'" Kids often learn more of lasting survival value to them at recess or at a "sleepover" than in a classroom.

Referring to these skills in his article, Brooks writes, "The traits that do make a difference are poorly understood, and can't be taught in any classroom." If by "taught" Brooks means delivered to students didactically, imparted to them the way so much of the academic curriculum has been traditionally delivered, I agree with him.

However, that does not mean that they cannot be learned in school. On the contrary, school is an ideal place for them to be learned. Indeed, where you have a controlled collection of children together in the same space for six to eight hours a day under the supervision of professional experts in human behavior, it's hard to think of a better delivery system. As Brooks is pointing out, these skills have as their foundation the rigors of social interaction—in fact, these are the skills for making social interaction successful.

School: a varsity sleepover led by professionals!

Recent research shows that we are born with the ability to know what someone else needs and try to help out. For instance: Man walks into a room with a clothesline across it, takes a handful of clothespins out of a basket and starts pinning up clothes. A mother and her eighteen-month-old son are sitting on the floor watching.

After pinning several items, the man accidentally drops a pin on the floor. He then pretends to reach over the clothesline to try to pick up the dropped pin, but his arms just aren't long enough. The eighteen-month-old watches the man struggle for few seconds, then leaves his mother, goes over to the clothespin, picks it off the floor, and holds it up to the man, who takes it and says thank you. The boy goes back to his mother on his own.

This and many moments like it have occurred under experimental situations in the last few years demonstrating that one of our culture's deeply held convictions—children are naturally selfish and have to be taught empathy—is false. Forty-some years of working with grade-school children have taught me the same thing.

The education profession is responding to the research about the skills necessary for success in the twenty-first century (as if they haven't always been essential skills.)

The most important twenty-first-century skill is still not on the list: to contribute. Most (but not all) schools in America were born locked within the mindset that "the cognitive," and "the social-emotional" are dichotomized. The former matters, but actually only academic expressions of cognitive activity really matter, and students are evaluated on progress toward these objectives. "The social-emotional" is a secondary consideration on the report card, if at all. Why?

In our belief system, being thoughtful of others is a virtue, but we don't actually believe in it. We *believe in* "individuality." We appreciate an act of kindness as we would a nice surprise dessert at the end of a meal, but we don't expect it as the meal, itself. Social responsibility is preached more than expected. Empathy, which is as wired into our brains at birth as balance and fear, is understood to be a rare commodity that only some people have, and something that has to be taught.

"Just be yourself" feels good but hangs in the air like the sound of one hand clapping. Selves don't exist in vacuums, and the notion that we can make ourselves happily independent of others is shocking in its myopia when you stop to think about it. It is also destructive to all those who keep trying. We can't make ourselves happy; millions have died trying. A cure for some depressions might be to devote yourself to the happiness of others.

When schools add "to contribute" to their list of essential skills, they get better results all around. When they decide that mattering is their mission, and make it their top priority, it changes how they do business and they turn out young people who have no use for bullying, cheating, arrogance, or any of the other symptoms of a dysfunctional community because they have the skills to harmonize their needs, values, and interests with those of others.

What if when kids came home from school, they could all tell a story about how they mattered today? What if that's what parents asked, for example, "What difference did you make, today?" I know. It sounds really hard to say, but why?

We want all our young people to be employable when the academic rat race is over. People who get the jobs and keep them, understand money as not only the reason for working, but also a symbol of their value to someone or to society.

The cause of most bad behavior, dropping out, and the other symptoms of American's failing school system, is that much of school does not serve the students' most fundamental need, the need to be valuable.

Children resist being managed, but they are happy to be led, especially if leadership helps them with their own leadership skills. Humans are herd animals, but there is a leader in each of us, and our wellbeing in life requires that we keep gaining competence in when, where, and how to lead. A life of pure followership is deadening. Sometimes it can be a killer.

No one is at fault that education is not happening in most school systems. Systems tend to be insensitive to the active ingredients of education: internal motivation, individual decision-making, useful data, specificity, unique characters collaborating and creating to make a difference, and love—most importantly, love.

Individuals could, however, take responsibility. System leaders could hold teachers accountable for what really matters. Teachers could be true to their calling. We, the people, could expect educators to educate rather than simply follow directions and sort children. It may seem like a management nightmare but that is the leadership challenge.

CHAPTER 17

Home Schooling Is an Oxymoron

I never let my schooling interfere with my education.

—Mark Twain

Sorting children begins in first grade. It was decided long ago that first grade was the correct time to teach reading. The sorting that schools do starts here. For "normal people" it is the right time to start. If you are already reading by age six-and-a-half, you are "gifted." If you are neurologically not ready to read, yet, you soon become categorized as "learning disabled." By second or third grade you are taken out of your classroom and sent to the "special ed" room. You and your classmates know that the "special ed" room is just a euphemism for the place where the dummies are sent.

This common practice is obviously flawed—criminally flawed—since the average age at with a child is neurologically ready to read may be six-and-a-half, but the range is ages three to nine. And almost all humans can learn to read. How soon you can read is rather unimportant if you are being educated in a school that educates.

Noticing a person's abilities is only half the project. Employing them so that the person is internally motivated to use this ability so that it is of value to others, is the other half. Neither success, nor happiness, nor thriving, nor longevity, nor any metric of a good life, is a function of ability, but a function of applied ability, response ability. If an ability exists in a vacuum, it doesn't exist (for all practical purposes).

Therefore, school should be less focused on ability and more focused on efficacy, and to be efficacious, one must be in a social environment. This is why the delivery system for education gravitates to something we call "school," and why a key factor in the quality of school is the quality of the social environment. If, for one reason or another, schooling must be done at home, the size and quality of the social group at home are important factors.

One day. Alicia, lead teacher of the Leaping Lizards, a class of twenty-four preschoolers, noticed that one of her four-year-olds, Tjaard, was showing signs of being ready to read. He would come into the classroom each morning and sound out words on the morning message board. She got him a few beginning reader books to see what he could read. Tjaard became really excited after he read his very first book and read it over and over and over again. She had him take it home and read it to his mom and dad.

The next day he came to school very excited and announced that his parents were surprised. Alicia encouraged Tjaard to read the book to his friends. After he read it to his buddies, she noticed that some of his buddies who would be going to kindergarten next year were a little surprised that Tjaard, who was younger, knew how to read before they did.

Before long they were having Tjaard read them a book every morning; from him they learned how to memorize what each page says, and then they "read" to other children as well. Before long there was a reading frenzy going on in the class!

In a leadership school, classes buddy up with other classes. First and fifth graders learn together on a regular basis.

One project is a letter-writing campaign, in which buddies send each other letters telling their buddy three facts about themselves and asking them three questions. One day they played a game in which one person said two facts and one fictional thing about themselves and the rest of the group had to guess what was fiction. Both first and fifth graders were amazingly good at determining fact from fiction. They also used a wide variety of techniques, both verbal and non-verbal, to fool the others.

These kinds of moments can occur in a school all day long, one hundred eighty days a year. Consider the educational objectives: not just reading and writing, but many higher-order thinking skills and, in fact, the full development of the whole child in ways that works for him or her.

Training can happen by one child working alone or with one adult or in front of a computer. But education, for best results, requires a community with enough individuals in it to create a critical mass that will result in enough interactions to challenge the entire organism to grow in all the many ways it needs to grow to be successful in an increasingly complex and changing world. For best results, education requires a school, and a good school is a collection of individuals with a common purpose.

Twenty years ago, I visited the lab school of UCLA and had a long talk with the assistant principal in charge of curriculum. She had just decided to leave schooling and get into curriculum development for a software company.

"School is obsolete," she said. "Kids can learn this stuff so much better and faster on computers." A challenging idea. At the time it was thought-provoking for me, so I thought about what she was saying. Just that month at my school one of the eighth graders had acquired some algebra software and worked through a whole year of algebra on the computer. Hmmmm.

"No," I finally said. "This would be true, if all we are doing is drilling on basic skills. One should probably just stay home and get some really good software but that is not all we are trying to do." (Today, of course, I would add, "Yes. If all we want is knowledge, just Google it.")

Maybe, this assistant principal had gotten burned out doing "schooling," but if school is an education, school is self-rewarding—it is fun—hard, maybe, but fun, too. And for schooling to be an education, social challenges are required.

The central reality is that human beings did not learn to survive on this planet by brute strength, or individual ingenuity, but by sticking together and learning from each other. Even if you wanted to claim that our genius as a species is our ability to design and develop technology, you would still be stuck with the reality that very few major technological advances or scientific discoveries were made by an individual acting alone.

The stories we tend to tell about heroes like Edison, leave out the fact that these heroes were usually a part of a team or in conversation with others about their work. Our advances, let alone our very survival, are the result of working together. For best results, we want one person's learning to have an impact on the learning of others and achieve an explosion of interactions—each person building on another's ideas. A human being acting alone is a very vulnerable creature.

WE EXIST IN RELATIONSHIP

Talking about their buddy projects, teachers go on about how collaboration between older and younger students brings out the best in everyone. "The fifth graders take their responsibilities so seriously. They love making a difference to the first graders." "They were amazed to see how fast and how clever the first graders are." "Yeah, and how delightful they are as people." "They are learning to put themselves in someone else's shoes." "So many kids discovered and appreciated strengths in other students."

Central to a creative culture is the understanding that we exist in relationship. Our relationships are essential to ourselves. We *are* our relationships. The kids know this. By age two, when empathy is blossoming, they begin learning that their friends are essential to who they are and that they have to harmonize their will with the wills of others to make those relationships work, sometimes even sacrificing felt-self-interest to find self-fulfillment.

There was a tense moment in preschool one April during an Easter egg-coloring activity. As each child was carefully protecting his eggs, waiting for the dyeing to begin, Kian suddenly cried out, "One of my eggs is cracked." Before the teacher could even respond to the potentially disastrous situation, Paolo piped up, "Here, you can have one of mine."

At a workshop for early childhood educators when I asked for examples of this phenomenon of young humans finding win-win solutions to social dilemmas, I was swamped with stories. It seems that dozens occur every day, and good teachers notice. Here's another one:

Aiden was a five-year-old who had been having trouble in his social relationships. Aidan's eighth-grade buddy, Samuel, was enormously helpful. The teacher overheard them talking once. "Samuel sounded like a member of the faculty. His relationship with Aidan was a powerful, stabilizing force. Knowing that his relationship was helpful to Aidan was, of course, of enormous value to Samuel, too."

Visitors are impressed when they attend an assembly where hundreds of students of all ages listen to one person talking without distracting each other with their own agenda. I was standing with a group of visitors once when three first graders even came up to me after one such assembly to apologize for talking while others were making announcements. We hadn't even noticed. Teachers in such schools are proud of how deferential and respectful students are to each other most of the time and know it's because the students are given responsibility.

In a discussion about rules in a seventh-grade class one year, Cara volunteered, "By following rules we gain trust and more freedom." (And Cara is no "goody-goody.") The recognition that each of us can benefit from the other and that we all benefit from the community to which we must be devoted for our own good is a major lesson a good school teaches constantly as a continuous part of the activity in and out of class.

It is true (as Polonius says to Laertes) that if we are true to ourselves, we cannot be false to anyone. However, for this to be true, there must be the recognition that the converse is also true: that being true to others is a good way to true to ourselves. Harmonizing what we want with what others want is essential for happiness. We cannot hurt others without hurting ourselves. And ultimately, we do not exist outside of the difference we make in the world. Sometimes it seems that the students know this better than the adults.

CHAPTER 18

The "Soft," "Non-cognitive Skills" are Hard, Cognitive, and Learned in Community

In Times of Crisis the Nomenclature Must Be Changed.

—Robert Parks

In a third-grade class in Johns Hill, a public magnet school in Decatur, Illinois, most of the children are at their desks writing, but one group of students who finished their work are sitting on the floor at the back of the room playing a game with twenty white dice each of which has a different word on each of its six faces. Bailey has just made a sentence: "The cute wife gave a soft laugh." But two of the other players dispute it as a valid sentence. Janice insists that "soft laugh" doesn't quite work. Henry, the scorekeeper tends to think Janice has a point and suggests that Bailey could make it work if it were "the soft wife gave a cute laugh." All four immediately agree and Henry puts a seven in Bailey's column on the scorecard.

Henry rolls the dice and starts a new sentence. Janice says, "The subject's fine, but what's the predicate?" All four of them suggest possibilities to Henry who eventually comes up with "I like to hear your face laugh" before the sand finishes running through the three-minute timer.

The game progresses gracefully through constant conflict:

"You can't flip the dice to other sides to find other words."

"I'll give you four for the first four words, because that's a sentence, but the rest doesn't make sense."

"Bailey's in the lead. 7 + 10 = 17."

"You don't know that; we haven't totaled everything yet."

The ability of these children to collaborate is remarkable. Rarely have I seen a group of adults disagree as often as these four eight-year-olds in such a friendly, mutually supportive way. Each child is a decision-maker in competition with three other decision-makers, and nobody gets mad.

Taking on challenges, controlling yourself, changing perspective, connecting, communicating, thinking critically, creative learning—these Seven C's are at least as important as the Three R's, and there's nothing "soft" or "non-cognitive" about them. It's time to call them the Hard Curriculum. The state tests evaluate schools based on the written curriculum, but life and the students evaluate a school on its ability to deliver the Hard Curriculum because the latter is what makes the difference between success and failure in life.

Whether the written curriculum uses the common core standards of the current educational reform effort or the No-Child-Left-Behind standards of the last one, doesn't really matter much, because mastering the Hard Curriculum does not depend on *what* is taught, but *how* it is taught. Moreover, you can't teach to this test because the pre-frontal cortex builds its capacity while engaged in self-directed, internally motivated, real-life problem-solving and decision-making.

Don't underestimate children under age fourteen. Treat them as if social responsibility is exactly what they are going for. Children are not naturally selfish barbarians who have to be taught empathy, morality, and civic mindedness. They have to be given the opportunity to be valuable to those around them—and are ready right away.

Let them clear the dinner table (age one-and-a-half), clean the floor (age two-and-a-half), go on a mission to the person next door (age six), write a letter to the Mayor of Oakland (age eight), set up the chairs in the multi-purpose room, get parents to stop smoking, teach younger kids, organize a group to clean up Lake Merritt and make a research project out of their question, "Where does all this litter come from?" (age five and up). It's an infinite list.

If this were what the world expects of children, then when their high school says they have to serve in a soup kitchen, they will either go enthusiastically because they're on a mission, or they will recommend a better mission to the administration. If, however, the world mistakes their self-centeredness for selfishness and narcissism, we will get what we expect.

Some changes that should be made tomorrow to improve the quality of the educational culture are: (1) all students of all ages would have at least one project they were working on to make a difference in the real world at all times, (2) people stop using the language of altruism (like "service,") and (3) keep our eye on self-actualization.

GENIUS, THE VOICE OF OUR CHARACTER, CALLS US INEXORABLY TOWARD OUR CALLING

The need to contribute is not on Abraham Maslow's pyramid of the needs that light the path to self-actualization. It should be. One does not have to be especially mature and/or enlightened to want to contribute to the lives of others. The opposite is true. You have to be especially disabled not to want to be valuable to others.

Genius, the voice of our character, calls us inexorably toward our calling—which includes the difference we make to others. We are not alone in this world.

CHAPTER 19

Social Deprivation Causes Cognitive Deprivation

Alone we can't do anything.

—Jane Goodall

On a tour of the Decatur Summer Camps, we ended at the Thomas Jefferson School Building in a classroom of twelve students who had "failed" their seventh-grade year. They stood in teams of three at tables that displayed complex paper constructions that rise three feet above the tabletops.

As we visitors walked from table to table, we were as impressed with their poise as with their construction. They spoke up to this group of adults with confidence and self-possession, articulately talking about what was unique and valuable about the model roller coasters they had made.

That their constructions actually worked was impressive, but even more impressive were their stories of the social challenges they had in building them, and how they resolved them. They talked about what they learned in the process.

When the teacher told us that collaboration was their biggest challenge because until now their elementary school had given them very little practice at it, I made him repeat it. "Yes," he said, "Elementary school has very little collaboration in it. There are almost no activities that required cooperation."

From what I have seen I would agree. Even though in many classrooms they often to sit four to a table, any interaction with their partner is almost always met with censure by the teacher. Traditionally, school is about each person doing his or her own work and striving on their own to measure up to standards.

No wonder these twelve young people had failed. School had failed them.

To find the root cause of this failure, look beyond the schools to the society they are supposed to feed. Listen to the conversation around us.

"I know Mr. Garfield does more harm than good. He never listens and he tries to bully other people with his ideas. But the thing is he is so smart."

How can we call Mr. Garfield and Graham smart when they are so bad at The Hard, Cognitive Curriculum?

Social deprivation causes cognitive deprivation because children are social scientists and need to practice their trade. Great teachers see their classroom as a social science lab for the children to experiment their way to high social competence.

My daughter, Katie, told the story of the year she and her classmates got organized—fifth grade. At lunchtime they noticed that they were sitting in different groups. Someone noticed and said: "Hey, how come we are sitting in separate groups?"

"Yeah, what's that all about?"

"Yeah, why don't we all sit together?"

"Let's form a club, Let's call it Kids Against Teachers."

"Yeah, KAT."

They were still talking about it as they came back into classroom. Noticing their enthusiasm for the subject, the teacher, Judy Stone, listened to what they were saying and had the mental flexibility to see that it was social studies. She said: "Okay What are you talking about."

"We formed a club."

"Yeah, KAT."

"What does KAT stand for," asked the teacher.

One smart ten-year-old said, "Kids Are Talking."

"Yeah, Kids Are Talking," said two other students in quick succession with smiles and knowing looks at each other.

"Well," said the teacher, "One of the things were are going to study this year is the U.S. Constitution. Would you like to write a constitution for your group?"

"Yes," said several kids.

Judy broke them up into committees to work on different parts of the project: writing a mission statement, making a list of rules and agreements, deciding on what positions they needed in the organization, and so on. For the rest of the afternoon until Physical Education they worked on the design of their organization. Later in the week, handmade signs appeared all over the school, one conspicuously right outside the principal's office.

When Judy told me about it, she said: "K.A.T. stands for Kids Are Talking. They are writing a constitution. It's really great. They have run into a snag. They already have a constitutional crisis. Their mission statement was 'Include Everyone.' Immediately, Kevin said, 'What if I want to sit by myself? What if somebody doesn't want to be included?'"

The inside story, that I got from Katie, is that first the organization was called: "Kids Against Teachers," but that they changed the name when they realized they needed their teacher to approve of their idea.

Walk through any school where good teaching is going on at any time of any day and one will see children making a difference: to their classmates, to younger children, to their teachers. If teachers think of their job as creating the conditions in which their students can make a difference, we will be awestruck by the sensitivity and articulateness of the children in school, warmed by the kindness shown by one student for another, thrilled by the works of art coming out of the art room, charmed by the complexity of child's play.

Doing something for someone else is often thought of as altruistic. Our society tends to dichotomize our actions into those that are selfish and those that are selfless. At a good school, children experience how service toward our community and toward our peers also serves ourselves. They experience mutuality.

As the world struggles toward being one global community, the law of mutuality becomes more and more obvious: to be good for me, it has to be good for everyone else; if it bad for other people, it's bad for me. This concept is at the core of an emerging world culture. Schools have some catching up to do.

I recently watched one third grader deal with his frustration toward a classmate who was struggling with a math problem. This third grader's demeanor changed entirely when he saw his fellow student's struggle as an opportunity and decided to help him out. Here was the chance to express sensitivity, to share learning, to help a friend's struggle, and in the process, to better himself, and he straightened up, a bit as he took on the challenge.

It's exciting to see how often children can seize these opportunities. Two preschoolers conflict over something they each want, and then, figure out how to get what they want *and* to be friends at the same time. Kindergartners and first graders learn that both the individual and the group suffer when everyone speaks at once. Small groups of second or third graders figure out how each can make a contribution to a common project.

A New Yorker cartoon shows a teacher at a blackboard with numbers on it: $2 + 2 = 4$, $5 - 3 = 2$, and $2 + 3 = 5$, and so on. The students are in their seats and one hand is up. The caption reads, "*Please, Ms. Sweeney, may I ask where you're going with all this?*"(14).

Where are you going with all this? Everyone gets the point. This is the same "schooling" that Mark Twain said would never interfere with his "education." Most American children are going through the motions. What is the game they are preparing for? They are like soccer players practicing drills without ever playing a game. For too many kids what goes on in school is actually ancillary to where they sense they need to be going.

At The Children's School in La Jolla, California, everyone DOES know where they are going. In a conversation with fifth graders, when I asked what is so great about the school, Lilly, the first to speak up said, "The teachers care where I am going in my career."

For twenty-five solid minutes her classmates followed with other concise articulations of what great education looks like. Statements like:

"Here the teachers help you understand things."

"The teachers here teach you the way you learn, not just the way they want to teach."

"The teachers listen to us."

"One teacher taught me not to be afraid of my mistakes."

"We work together on projects."

"We get to be creative."

"We get to help out little kids."

When I said, "It sounds like you feel trusted, here. Raise your hand if you feel trusted," all the hands went up.

These ten year olds know what education is and are very happy to be experiencing it.

Two days in the school brought me nearly to tears seeing how self-possessed, poised, and generous the students were. Conflicts between students were quick educational moments because everyone is trained in seeing conflicts as learning opportunities.

IT SOUNDS LIKE YOU FEEL TRUSTED HERE.

The seventh and eighth graders talked freely about how they have relationships with everyone in the school from preschoolers to teachers to administrators. Students regularly research problems and make recommendations to adults.

In one room, third graders were presenting their research findings on rivers of the world to the class. They were as poised in their responses to correction as they were in presenting what they knew.

Everyone is on the same mission. Students speak up and leave room for others to speak. They advocate for themselves, for others, for truth, and for justice.

Adults say things like: "We focus our energies on helping them learn how to work together." "The learning is designed around meaningful projects." "It's a safe place to be yourself." "The students take turns leading the community meeting every Friday and present what they are learning to the whole school including parents." "All the children are comfortable with public speaking."

I asked one parent, "Does everyone here understand the connection between public speaking and high academic achievement?"

"I don't know, but I do," she said. "To stand up in front of a group of people and talk, you have to know what you know and understand it so you can answer questions and not be afraid to be wrong and make mistakes. Public speaking is the final exam of education. If someday they find themselves having to defend their PhD thesis, they will find they've done it all their lives."

The teachers in this school seem to understand that self-control, perspective taking, connecting, collaborating, communicating, critical thinking, and love of learning are the mental abilities central for success.

Moreover, the teachers are acting as if they know that all children have a need to contribute and that this need to contribute fuels their development of these other seven abilities.

From a very early age children seem to know instinctively what the world will require of them and, like Lilly, are passionate about being valuable in it. We humans are wired to find our place in a group. In fact, we owe our large brain and sophisticated decision-making cortex to the fact that our branch of the primate line learned that collaboration had great survival value and therefore got serious about working the very challenging problems of collaboration.

The students know that the teachers know where they are going: creating the conditions for student success in life. The Children's School is showing that when schooling is an education, school bullying is not even an issue. When children are making something of themselves, making a difference, and contributing, education doesn't get any better than this.

My hyper-energetic three-year-old grandson, Musa, helped me empty the dishwasher and sets the table for dinner on his own. Dishes are kept in cabinets at his level. We've learned to anticipate. When he's about to go haywire, we give him a challenging job.

As soon as his little brother Ilyas was able to walk at the age of nineteen months, he took over the job of clearing the table. Now he had a goal. When he was finished eating, he would ask to get down from the table and begin to take the empty dishes we gave him to the kitchen. He gets mad if we do his job for him.

Children want to make a difference. What should we expect from children if we don't give them constructive opportunities to do so?

CHAPTER 20

Perfectionism Is Another Disability

You treated us as if we knew what we were doing.

—Anola Picket, Middle School Teacher

Making schools a safe place to make mistakes not only helps to create a learning culture; it also prepares children to be successful in life. Scientists learn as much from mistakes as from successes. He who learns the most wins.

The little commuter flight from Decatur to Chicago (the first leg of my trip) was one of those tiny airplanes with eight seats. The four seats in the middle faced each other, and I happily found myself in a one-hour discussion about education with three other interesting people.

MAKE AS MANY MISTAKES AS YOU CAN.

At one point in the conversation a forty-five-year-old CEO of a big Canadian company sitting across from me said: "When people ask me how you get to be CEO, I tell them, it's not what you think. It's not about getting good grades and graduating from a great business school.

"I say it's about making mistakes. It's about working hard for what you want and not being afraid to fail. I made as many mistakes as I could.

"By the time I was forty I had made as many mistakes as the average eighty-year-old. So I was as smart and as skilled and as wise as an eighty-year-old. My competence was obvious, and so they gave me the job.

"But most of all you won't be afraid of anything and will therefore be more likely to make more decisions, and so your decisions will get better and better."

Children know this. Continuous, enthusiastic struggle to learn is what happiness and success look like to children. Adults call it "playing."

Maintaining this attitude throughout life is the secret to a happy and successful life. The goal of an effort is not its value; the value of an effort is the education one gets when trying to achieve it.

WHAT IF WE EVALUATED TEACHERS BY COUNTING THE NUMBER AND KINDS OF DECISIONS STUDENTS MAKE EVERY DAY?

All challenges are opportunities to build our executive self and to develop our skills of self-control, connecting, perspective taking, critical thinking, communicating, collaborating, facing a challenge, and learning. If you are afraid of making mistakes, you'll have a hard time taking on these challenges that result from your decisions. It's easier for children because they are less resistant to changing their minds. It helps if our executive self can remember that it has a partner, an inner resource, an inner child.

As we send our kids off to school, we should not wish for them success. We should not envision their hands in the air dying to be called on so they can give the right answer time after time. We should not wish that their classroom is peopled with all friends and no bullies. We don't send our kids to school for it to be easy; we should want it to be hard. If it were easy, there would be no point to school in the first place.

So actually, the formula for success is the same as the formula for good education, a formula for turning out people who can think well in the classroom, the science lab, the workplace, the home . . . everywhere: Decision-making yields mistakes → yields thoughtfulness → yields knowledge → yields authority→ yields better decisions→ yields more mistakes. It's the way humans are wired to learn. The essential ingredient for making this formula work is valuing the truth over the results. Each decision is an experiment, the testing of a hypothesis.

By contrast, following directions to find right answers yields thoughtlessness and powerlessness. The kind of thinking that is essentially "Guess what's in the teacher's head" is classically memorialized in the movie *Ferris Bueller's Day Off* by the history teacher droning: "Anyone? Anyone?" We laugh in horror; then we forget. What if we evaluated teachers by counting the number and kinds of decisions students make every day?

Mark

I told the CEO the story about Mark, a friend of mine who is now the head of a big K-12 school in North Carolina. He was thirty when he became head of his first school. He had taken an unsuccessful school and made it a success. He hired me as his leadership coach when he had been in that position five years. One day Mark said: "I've got this job knocked. At first, I was so nervous that I didn't know what I was doing, that I didn't have the ability or the training to do the job. Then I finally figured it out. Everybody wanted me to make decisions. So I just started making decisions. At first my decisions were only 50 percent good. But it didn't matter. If I made a bad decision, that just gave me the opportunity to make another decision, and then another and another. It wasn't long before I was making mostly good decisions. But it didn't matter—other people had permission to make decisions and make mistakes, so more and more we had a whole community of people who were making decisions. We went from being a bad school to being an awesome school inside of two years."

That reminded me of what one of my former teachers told me when I went back to visit her in my old school.

She had said, in a conspiratorial whisper, "You did a great job."

"What did I do right?" I asked.

"You treated us as if we knew what we were doing."

CHAPTER 21

Staying out of Trouble Is Not a Worthy Mission

You do not have to be good.
You do not have to walk on your knees
for a hundred miles through the desert repenting.

—Mary Oliver

Quite often, students believe that their job at school is to do well, to prepare for the future, to stay out of trouble. They are sometimes quite surprised to discover that their responsibility is to learn.

I was talking with a first-grade girl the other day who had been "sent" to my office. I discovered that she did not understand the word "responsibility." She said that responsibility was about doing what you were supposed to do. I said no, it is about making your own decisions, about deciding what you want and getting it.

I asked her to write down what she wanted, and she wrote: "I want to do the right things so that I won't get into trouble."

WHAT ARE YOU HERE FOR: STAYING OUT OF TROUBLE OR LEARNING?

I said, "Ah, ha! Now I understand. You don't understand what your job is here. You are trying to stay out of trouble and that's not what I want you to do. I want you to do what you want to do."

Her eyes got big. She couldn't believe it. "Really?" she said.
"Yes."

I told her to write a list of what she wanted to do at school, and she wrote: learn, make friends, play on the roof, do math, reading and writing, and work in centers.

"That is great," I said. "Now these are your responsibilities," and I took the paper, and wrote across the top in big capital letters: "SUZY'S RESPONSIBILITIES," with arrows pointing down. I said, "These are your responsibilities, and nothing else."

Now, I never learned if this intervention had impact on this child, but, in my thirty-four years of experience as head of a school, I have seen that, when children understand that learning, and only learning, is what is expected of them, they become so busy learning that the rest does, indeed, take care of itself.

We decided to spell this out for our students in the student handbook:

1. Be the self you want to be.
2. Value mistakes as learning opportunities. Don't be afraid to make them, but try to fix them and learn from them.
3. Don't avoid conflict; make it a learning experience.
4. Collaborate. Let others know what you know and let them teach you what you need to learn.
5. Take responsibility (all or nothing; not fifty-fifty)

Notice how countercultural these principles are. Most schools make children think that the worst thing they can do is make a mistake, that we want peace and conflict is bad, and that they should keep their eye on their own paper and that helping classmates is cheating.

We say, value mistakes and learn from them. We say learn from conflict. We don't pit students against each other in a contest to see who comes out on top, we tell them to share what they know: how to give and receive criticism.

Vibrato

To listen with an open heart, means to listen with a willingness to change.

—Tim Mollak

Jonah, age two, stood at the block table in the Frick Museum in Nashville piling up blocks trying one combination after another. It looked like he was playing "Blockhead," except that rather than piling them up one at a time, he held two blocks together, then tried to put them on top of the first stack of two. He tried all different combinations of shapes—two rectangles end to end, a square and a triangle, a flat and a cylinder, and so on.

What neural networks was he building? Did he have a vision? Was he exploring the properties of each shape? Was he working on his eye-hand coordination? Was he exploring the relationship between the geometric center of an object and its center of gravity? From watching children over the years my guess is: "all of the above."

One thing was obvious: his brain loved those blocks. He worked for half-an-hour—long past when his parents were done with blocks and ready to move on to the next activity.

I wanted to help. As an experienced block builder, I could have told him that this two-at-a-time method was the hard way of building something. I could have shown him how to put one on top of the other carefully so that the base was more stable. I could have explained that to be stable the center of gravity has to be below the geometric center. But even I am not that stupid. The challenge he had set for himself was driven by inner neurological necessity. He was going for something, and I was smart enough not to presume to know what it was. I just watched.

It can be frustrating for a father to watch his son try to do something. From an adult point of view we are presiding over failure after failure. But if the goal is to build strong brains, we simply must let the brain direct the project.

At four in the morning, Barbara lies in her bed going over and over all of the ways she tried and failed to get Johnny to learn that 25 - 16 = 9.

That same morning Mark, the principal, can't get back to sleep thinking about the sexist thing the top candidate for third-grade teacher said in his office the day before.

Barry sits at his typewriter staring at the words on the paper in front of him.

They all realize they made a mistake somewhere.

How well these four people do in life depends in large part on their attitude toward mistakes. Barbara was considering calling the parents in to discuss Johnny's difficulties and to recommend a thorough psycho-educational evaluation. Mark was considering hiring the teacher, anyway. Barry was about to rip the paper out and start again. Jonah? Right. He didn't have a problem. For him mistakes were all part of the research and the building of his brain. To a scientist a wrong answer is as interesting as a right answer. Each one provides the same amount of data.

An expert violinist puts her finger on a string, presses it to the sounding board, and draws the bow over the string. She does not expect that the finger is in the perfect place; for she knows that making the right sound requires vibrating the finger above and below the correct string length many times a second. It's called vibrato. Similarly, good decision-making is not a set of one-shot actions, but a vibrato of a series of decisions.

Life for humans is effort and error. No matter how good one gets, one still makes mistakes. Achievement isn't getting it right; it's successive approximation, like the musical concept of vibrato when you are trying to hit a note. Paradoxically, all four people get better results when they realize the name of the game is building a brain.

CREATING, TEACHING, LEADING, AND WRITING ALL HAVE ONE THING IN COMMON: THE NUMBER OF TRIALS MATTERS MORE THAN THE NUMBER OF ERRORS.

The next day Barbara tried something new. She asked Johnny to explain his decision-making process to her. He showed her how he would do 25 - 16 and came up with 9. Even though it seemed circuitous to her, she congratulated him on showing her a new way. Johnny then proceeded to do a whole worksheet of double-digit subtraction.

Mark once said to me: "I was half-way through my second year as principal, when I finally understood what my job was. People aren't counting on me to be right; they are counting on me to make decisions. As soon as I realized that, I had the job knocked: just make decisions. If I make a wrong decision, guess what; I make another decision, and then another and another. A mistake is simply an opportunity to make another decision."

This time Mark decided not to hire the teacher but to continue the search even though the rest of the hiring committee loved the candidate. He turned hiring a teacher into an opportunity for him to communicate where he stood on a critical diversity issue.

Barry ripped out the paper and started over again.

Creating, teaching, leading, and writing all have one thing in common: what is critical is not the number of errors but the number of trials.

If schools were really focused on preparing students for success, they would keep track of the number of trials rather than the number of errors. If a school is to graduate the leaders it must by placing a higher value on the courage to make decisions than on being right. If we want our young people to be good at making lemonade out of lemons, we have to give them a lot of practice at it: all day long, day after day after day. We should all give points for making decisions rather than for making the "right" decision.

Would This Happen at a School Near You?

Creativity is allowing yourself to make mistakes.
Art is knowing which ones to keep.

—Scott Adams

One of the parents at my last school emailed me after dropping her son Harry off at school on the first day. "You would have been so proud," she wrote. "On the way to school this morning, I asked Harry what he was looking forward to in second grade. You know what he said? He said: 'My mistakes.'"

I did indeed accept the pat on the back. It made me feel I had been a successful headmaster. It's all about creating a culture in which it is a safe place to be your imperfect self and to make mistakes.

"What are you looking forward to in school this year?"

"My mistakes."

That was my final exam.

Perfectionism is a learning disability, because it leads to avoidance of mistakes, and avoiding mistakes compromises learning in very serious ways. A school where the children are proud of their mistakes is a school where perfectionism is low, and a school where perfection is low is likely to have less bullying.

> A parent comes into the classroom in the morning with her child in tow and says to the teacher, "We had a little trouble with our homework." That parent is compromising the child's education by relieving him of responsibility and teaching that being successful is more important than uncovering the truth.

Last week I met with a parent from my last school over a cup of coffee. She said, "Of all the things you said and wrote as head of our school, the one that keeps coming back to me most was your talk at the opening assembly of your last year at Children's Day School. I will never forget your words at the end of your opening remarks! At least, this is what I remember you saying: 'We love you. Your teachers love you; I love you; we all do. You are very loved children. Just remember that doesn't mean we will be easy on you. In fact it means the opposite. Loving you means that we will be hard on you.'"

"Your parents are not sending you here for us to make it easy for you. They want us to challenge you. If we do our job right, you will struggle. You will make mistakes. You will have conflicts. You will fail, and at Children's Day School, we think that is good. We want you to make as many mistakes as you can and learn from them. We believe you can handle it."

"I was looking at the children while you spoke, and when you said, '*We will be hard on you,*' I saw the student body sort of rise—literally. Their heads came up higher, they sat up straighter and there was pride in their faces. With my three girls I keep finding moments when I need this reminder."

"Your last first assembly was your best."

CHAPTER 22

The Need to Contribute Is a Childish Impulse

Strive not to be a success, but rather to be of value.

—Albert Einstein

Humans are born givers; those who never unlearn it die happy after a successful life. To treat others as if this is not true is an insult—an assault on their dignity. That this needs to be said is a reflection on a culture that, instead, assumes selfishness, celebrates independence, and rewards "individual achievement" over collective action. Such a culture is an affront to our humanity, because we are wired to be valuable to others.

In our culture, we tend to see children as dependent creatures whose steady march toward independence peaks in adolescence and who, after making money and raising a family, begin feeling the need to "give back" to society. Contributing is something we might do after we have made it on our own.

"Making it on our own!" Now there's a concept! That will never happen; it never has. A self-made man is an oxymoron. No one has ever made it on his own, and yet, we talk as if it were possible. Interdependence is not part of the end game of life if we get lucky. Interdependence is a life-long reality for most mammals. It is obvious in children, if we simply keep our eyes open.

The eight stages of psycho-social development outlined by renown psychologist Erik Erickson[1] leave us with the impression that all humans move from trust to autonomy to initiative to industry to identity to intimacy and only in the later years reach the seventh stage of "generativity"—that time of life when you feel that your life makes a difference and that you are leaving, as Wordsworth put it, "Footprints in the sands of time."

Chapter 22

THE NEED TO CONTRIBUTE IS AS PRIMARY AND FUNDAMENTAL A NEED AS SECURITY AND NUTRITION.

Abraham Maslow's pyramid,[2] his hierarchy of needs benchmarking the path to self-actualization, might lead us to believe that one has to be especially mature and/or enlightened to want to contribute to the lives of others.

The opposite is true. Fifty years of working with children—and in fact with teachers, parents and children of all ages—has taught me that the need to contribute is a fundamental human need. You have to be especially disabled not to want to be valuable to others. Research on babies shows that they are as wired to give as to receive. The need to contribute is as primary and fundamental a need as security and nutrition.

Children learn more when their work matters. Looking at children through this lens can bring new insights to how we construct our social environments, how we lead our lives, and how we can lead so as to create great moments for ourselves and others.

How to behave in public is something the students at St. Paul's Episcopal School in Oakland, California, learn and practice on their two-block walk to the park for lunch, recess, and physical education. (Right, it's true. It doesn't rain much in California.) This hike to the park has been going on for years and the students are in good habits. Halfway on their journey the children pass a sidewalk café and, of course, are too engrossed in each other and the social dynamics to pay much attention to what goes on there.

One day, however, they noticed something new on their journey. Over the vacation, the owners had built a low wall with planters on top separating the sidewalk from the tables, and in each planter were white pebbles right at a child-friendly height. To children, especially tweens with their minds on more important things, white pebbles are irresistible, and before long the route from the school to the park was marked by little white pebbles just like Hansel and Gretel's crumbs. The pebbles, of course, went right up to the school door incriminatingly.

The teachers and the principal were on it in a flash, of course, speaking to the students in their classes. Punishments were meted out to pupils persisting in picking pebbles. But none of this adult activity had any effect. Students could not resist the allure of the pebbles.

One day, sixth-grade teacher Susan Porter decided that it would be a good activity for her class to pick up pebbles. However, Susan is the kind of teacher who never wants to waste a teachable moment. When the pebbles arrived back in class, and the students were all seated at their tables—four to a table—Susan said: "As you know, we have a problem with kids taking the pebbles from the café. I don't think they are trying to be mean, but maybe they don't understand the situation fully. So my question for you to figure out today is: how long will it take for the pebbles in the planters to be all gone?

"What should we do first?"

Someone said, "First, let's find out how many pebbles there were on the sidewalk," and after some discussion it was agreed. Each table of students counted how many they had found, the numbers were written on the white board and then added.

"What is the volume of the pebbles we collected today?" was the next question. The students were on it in a flash. Using various containers of measurable size, the volume of each collection was calculated. A representative brought their pebbles to a large container in the center of the room, and one student computed the volume of the pebbles collected that day.

"Now we have to measure the volume of the planters at the restaurant," said Flo.

"Well, there is still plenty of time before you have to go to music, so let's go now," said Susan, and off they went to the restaurant armed with meter sticks to measure the planters. Back in class they calculated those volumes, and got to work on their estimates. Not all the tables came up with the same answer, but it didn't take long for them to resolve their differences.

Before anyone could even ask the ultimate question again, Darya blurted out, "Two-and-a-half months. All the pebbles in the planters will be gone in two-and-a-half months." After some discussion and calculation in their small groups, all agreed: two-and-a-half months.

"We should tell the school," said Thomas, and they all quickly agreed. They voted on their representatives. Colin was elected, it was decided that runner-up Mikaela, should go with him. (Twelve-year-olds do everything in pairs.)

Each student wrote what they thought the speech to the eighth graders should say and handed the drafts to Colin and Mikaela for their consideration.

Shanna finished her message early and decided that the kindergarten message should be worded differently, so she wrote another one to them. When she presented her idea to the class, they said they liked it but said, "The kindergarten is not part of the problem," and agree that it would be counterproductive to talk to them.

They made appointments to speak to the classes and did the next day. The trail of pebbles never reappeared. Problem solved in two class periods.

Adult Culture

In a true Leadership Community the culture of the classroom is reflected in the culture among the adults.

Dan's team of teachers was tired by the time it came to plan the April vacation camp program. Dan knew it would be hard to find volunteers—everyone needed the vacation, themselves. Nonetheless, he put "Staffing for Vacation Camp" on the agenda for their weekly meeting. When this item came up on the agenda, Dan said: "So, is there anyone who wants to work this vacation?"

Dan's question was greeted by a ten-second eternity of silence. Then Melissa spoke up: "I'll do Monday."

Then Mike said: "I'll do Tuesday," and in the next minute all the slots were filled.

With a smile on his face and gratitude in his voice Dan said: "What a different kind of union we have created. Thank you."

When is self-sacrifice self-fulfillment? When Self makes that decision.

A leader gets that kind of decision when he or she has created a team, a community, a band of brothers and sisters. Serving others is the *only* way to serve self—contrary to common American individualistic culture. Serving self at the expense of others leaves the most critical piece of self in limbo (or worse). When everybody is "looking out for number one," everyone experiences the deficit.

However, this is a cultural flaw rather than "the way people are." Our language distracts us from the truth. We talk as if we are "torn between self and other" as between "bad and good." Being "altruistic" is "morally responsible," but not necessarily in our own self-interest. Whether to do for others or to do for yourself is understood as a moral dilemma.

The choice is not a dilemma—there is only one self-serving choice. Doing things for others (even to the point of self-sacrifice) inherently fulfills self.

As Jill Bolte Taylor, discovered personally on December 10, 1996, when the left hemisphere of her brain went "offline" due to a hemorrhage, we have two brains. A left-brain that says: "I am myself, distinct, unique, independent," and a right brain that says: "I am my relationships." Fulfillment, happiness, success (etc.) are about integrating these two brains, and results in the discovery that, indeed, I am my relationships.

The confusion in our language is reinforced in the duality built into some religious traditions. Competition between our good selves and our bad selves is a dysfunctional cultural construction, not the way humans are naturally designed. This is why war heroes consistently report that their act of self-sacrifice was nothing special—they were just being themselves. The Rotarian slogan "service over self?" has it slightly wrong. Service *is* self.

Given half a chance, children show that altruism is the natural tendency. Want to get a three-year-old eating out of the palm of your hand? Show him how he can help you. Want to see a happy elementary school student? Ask him to help you with a challenging task. Want those "self-centered" middle-schoolers to behave responsibly? Give them the job of taking care of, or teaching, or just being with younger children. "Being yourself" is impossible in a social vacuum. Self has to make a difference.

We create our own hell when we act as if others are selfish or act as if our neighbors are not a part of our community. We create a heaven when decide to act as if making a difference to others is what makes everybody somebody, and that everyone is part of our community whether we have seen them before or not. The power for creating these heavens resides in our soul; this soul has a voice we can listen for in others; children often show us; we do well to notice.

CHAPTER 23

Building an Organization on the Need to Contribute

I see every unused ability in my class as an incipient behavior problem.

—Beth Campbell, kindergarten teacher

All good elementary school teachers know it is wise to try to use all of the capabilities of all your students. In this spirit it is good to remember that a human being who has been alive in our complex world for fifteen months has been working on her social capabilities for about ten thousand hours. By kindergarten that number jumps to over forty-three thousand.

Monica employed this wisdom brilliantly once with Timmy, a second grader who had trouble reading social cues and knowing how to handle himself with others. Although Timmy solved academic problems with ease, social problem-solving was enormously challenging. There was rarely a game of tag that didn't reduce him to tears. A disagreement with a classmate would turn to anger.

Talking about her frustrations to the principal one day, Monica said, "I have a very challenging class. I have Timmy on one end of the spectrum, and on the other I have Amanda, whose emotional stability and social skills are off the top of the charts."

Monica was back in the office at 7:45 the next morning. Eyes brimming with enthusiasm, she said, "I had this crazy thought when I woke up this morning. The first thought that popped into my head was: 'Make Amanda Timmy's social coach.'"

"I know it's a crazy idea, but I was thinking I could find the time to take Amanda aside today and talk to her about Timmy and see how she understood him, and how she felt about him, and how she felt about the idea of taking Timmy under her wing—in a way that was not too obvious—you know, be there for him at recess, go over and sit next to him when it looked like he was going to go off, or if he was having a conflict with someone, or, you know, . . . I don't know, is this crazy? I could . . ." Monica's eyes! She was on fire.

"Absolutely," said the principal. "Do it."

Amanda, of course, loved the idea—she was just the person—and she took on the responsibility with ease and grace.

She didn't change Timmy. He continued to have emotional outbursts and social challenges, but he relaxed. For the second half of the year when there was a problem, there was something that could be done. By using the abilities of a student, Monica turned a common classroom problem into learning opportunities for all.

Furthermore, Timmy was no longer upsetting the class or his teacher. Most importantly, second grade became a safe place for Timmy to be his own imperfect self, which was one giant step toward the class being safe place for everyone to be their own imperfect selves.

LETTING GO OF OUR MINDSETS AND LISTENING TO THAT VOICE INSIDE US.

If a teacher's job is to turn her class into a learning organization, it has to get organized. As Jim Collins writes in *Good to Great*, a leader's job is not only to get "the right people on the bus," but also to get them in "the right seats on the bus." Like leaders of regiments, leaders of classes usually do not have the luxury of getting "the right people on the bus"; they are stuck with the people they get. They can, however, put them in the right seats on the bus, and get them to work together.

Getting a group to work together is often a matter of making sure that there are no unused abilities. Coming up with creative solutions to difficult problems requires letting go of our mindsets and listening to that voice inside us that keeps having those crazy ideas. This is one of the secrets of great teachers and great leaders; it is also the secret of a successful and happy life.

CHAPTER 24

Diversity: The Solution, Not the Problem

Diversity: the art of thinking independently together.

—Hillary Clinton

In our culture, "Diversity" is understood to be a question of ethics, equity, and social justice. Diversity is understood as a moral good, and therefore, an issue of social, political, and economic justice. But in the interest of designing educational cultures, diversity is more than a moral good; it is essential. Diversity and the disciplines related to mobilizing diversity for the benefit of the group are some of the same disciplines required to maximize student performance.

"Celebrating" diversity is only a first step, facing up to the morality of diversity, working for social justice are all important. But the core value of diversity is that it helps build better brains. Rising to the cognitive, social, and emotional challenges of wrestling with our differences without fracturing our communities makes us smarter. Avoiding them makes us stupider.

The core concept of diversity work is that each person is unique; each person needs to be educated as if that uniqueness is a critical consideration; each person has a right and an obligation to define themselves and not be defined by another person or by the society they are in; and each person can make valuable contributions that are expressions of all that is inside them.

A basic assumption in cultures of diversity is that we differ, which means that we will be in conflict, which means that we will have to make conflict creative. Being inclusive is only the first step. Finding and drawing out our differences is the business of a school committed to diversity; for we all are helping each of us find the value that we each can add. A cultural of diversity and an educational culture are two names for the same thing.

Diversity flows in the fountain we drink from every day. In such cultures, for instance, our starting point is the assumption that we come to the table biased. In a culture of diversity, we work to understand how others see the world, and give them what *they* want rather than what we would want, or what we want them to want, or what we think they should want. People do as must asking and listening as telling and talking. People understand the value of not agreeing on a consensus until the quiet person has been asked what they think.

Normally, when people ask questions like, "What is the diversity of your school?" the answer is usually something like: "10 percent Asian, 10 percent black, 10 percent Hispanic, and 65 percent white." (Oh, and 5 percent "other.") But think about it. How gross is that? The truth is that there is as much diversity within each of these categories as there is between them. If you decide that this particular difference matters, you will end up violating most of your educational principles.

Categorizing children distorts reality in very destructive ways. If there are eight billion brains in the world, there are eight billion *kinds* of brains; each of us has a unique set of gifts and talents; we all learn differently; and the "normal" person doesn't exist.

A class with twenty-five students has twenty-five different kinds of learners, and to maximize the potential of each student they need to be taught as if they are. Once you have categorized kids, you have begun your trek down the wrong road—compromising everyone's education. Worse: once a student has categorized herself, she has limited herself. Carol Dweck's research shows that the categories in our heads are powerful predictors of our performance.

Categories are also powerful determiners of how we treat others. If we talk about "people with ADHD," for instance, our behaviors will be reactions to the understandings packed into this mindset rather than acting in the present, present to the unique human being in our presence. If we keep talking as if there are three kinds of people—gifted, normal, and disabled— teachers and parents will keep talking and acting as if it were true, even though it is obviously crazy.

People locked in ability-ist mindsets are in the sorting business, not the education business or the leadership business. If you are committed to bringing out the best in others, you love the unique weirdness of each person, love the marvelous diversity in each classroom, and organize your work around the self-actualization of each individual. And followers follow a lot better if they feel the person they are following cares about their unique character, their genius, their soul.

No two Asians are alike; no two dyslexics are alike; no two women are alike, and each of us (*of course*) needs to be treated the way we want to be treated—as the unique person we are. Learning organizations have transcended "The Golden Rule," and moved on to "The Platinum Rule:" *Treat other people the way THEY want to be treated rather than the way you would want to be treated.* They might care about something you don't care about, and vice-versa.

In a good school, each person feels it is safe place to be their imperfect self. This is essential for maximizing all of our educational objectives including test scores. In a culture of diversity, all the psychic energy people commonly put into measuring up, fitting in, and wondering if we are good enough and will go into collaborating, creating, contributing, and learning how to lead.

A true commitment to diversity makes a school a safe place for each of us to be ourselves. Correction. A commitment to diversity makes a school a safe place to transcend ourselves, listen to our genius, and build relationships with the genius in others.

For optimal brain development, we humans need to keep facing up to the challenge of people who are different from us. Diversity is an essential component of a school culture that serves social, emotional, and cognitive development.

Friends and Enemies

We hear a lot about the importance of parents and teachers working together, and especially what parents can do to prepare children for school. Well, children rise (or fall) to the high (or low) expectations we have of them. Are they given responsibility for the climate of the classroom at school? Or the tenor of the conversation at the dinner table? If we want them to be responsible, we have to give them opportunities to be responsible. Treat children as if they are already capable of real work in the world.

One evening at dinner a mother said to her sixth-grade daughter, "Cici, your class is such a wonderful class. You all seem so happy and are so good at working with each other."

She answered as if she was being asked a question, "Oh, that's easy. Everyone wants to be Abby's friend, and Abby doesn't exclude anyone."

Such a simple answer to one of the biggest questions for all of us: "How can we have environments where we all want to go to work every day."

"That's wonderful," said her Mom.

But then Cici said, "Yeah, and I am glad I am not in the seventh grade."

"Really? Why?"

"Because there is a girl in the seventh grade named Alison. Everyone wants to be Alison's friend, and Alison *does* exclude people. Likes being the queen bee and doesn't care if others get hurt."

Indeed, the seventh grade had a reputation in the school as "the mean girl" class.

It's normal to think, "A friend is someone we like," and "of course, not everyone can be friends." But if our mission is to prepare young people for the world today, then friendship skills are the most basic of basics. Being a friend to everyone has to be a norm rather than an impossible ideal.

Quaker Schools (there are ninety-two across the country) have this concept at the core of their culture, of course. Their modern name is Friends Schools. Being friendly to those we like is easy, but creating a friendship with anyone requires mental work of the hardest kind. Minds that can do this are not "soft." Learning the skills of treating everyone as if they are a friend is actually central to building creative brains that can create new and useful things and build working relationship that solve problems for the common good.

In most schools, teachers talk to kids about "values," "character," and "empathy," trying hard to teach kids to be responsible. In leadership cultures, the children develop their critical thinking, their communication, and their cooperative skills as they wrestle day to day with the fundamental challenges of differing with other people. After all, isn't this the key challenge of being human?

Don't Compartmentalize the Brain

How to be friendly with someone who is not your friend, how to increase your circle of friends without making enemies? How do you solve conflict so that the person with whom you differ does not become your enemy?

The mental work necessary for solving these common problems are not radically different from the thinking necessary for addressing academic problems—reading the situation, describing the problem, analyzing it, seeing different points of view, communicating clearly, listening, creating a synthesis, trying again—these are the kinds of things educated people can do, and therefore, what school is for.

The thinking required to solve a social problem is vastly more complex and challenging than most math problems. Understanding good literature and writing good stories requires utilizing the whole brain. Noticing how fictional characters develop their character is an important part of developing your character. Learning how characters in history became who they were and learning what became of them and their impact on the progress of the human race is obviously equally important for whole-brain development.

None of this "book learning" is a "purely rational" project. In fact, research with brain damaged people reveal that, indeed, if any of the emotional part brain is compromised, a person's decision-making is compromised (Tony Damassio). There is no such thing as a "purely rational" decision. A rational person whose reasoning is divorced his emotional system through brain damage, makes bad decisions or can't make any decision at all. If a person keeps making bad decisions, is it correct to call him intelligent?

Therefore, parents and teachers must get on the same page about social-emotional development. "Solves social problems" must be on the report card side-by-side with "solves math problems."

To graduate more Abby's and fewer Alison's maximizing friends and minimizing enemies must be an educational objective, not just a social objective. Diversity and inclusion are high values in educational cultures. Furthermore, kindness and respect must be more than just "values." Treating all people kindly and being respectful at all times no matter what must be laws. And here's a creative idea: what if "Brings out the best in others" were a metric?

Compartmentalizing book learning from "the social-emotional" compromises our ability to teach all skills. More importantly, it takes the students' focus off the priority of learning from social challenges thus creating less socially safe environments, thus compromising the kind of risk taking necessary for optimizing *all* learning, thus depressing test scores even for those students who can compartmentalize. Even the "smart kids" would better off if all parts of their brain were growing in tandem.

If we understand the skills for success, then proficiency at getting the family happily out of the house in the morning is just as important as completing homework. Teamwork at home is as important as the "homework."

The mission statements of most schools includes something like: "to educate children to be active, aware citizens with the skills and knowledge to participate meaningfully in the diverse and challenging new century." What distinguishes the leadership cultures from dysfunctional schools is whether or not they take this mission statement seriously and organize their habits, disciplines, rituals, and practices around it.

In good schools:

1. Character is not a separate subject, but understood to be at the heart of the work of each class.
2. Cognitive performance, social competence, and emotional intelligence are understood as intimately intertwined and not separated out as different zones of responsibility.
3. Diversity is understood as both a reality, and a desirable reality in that it is necessary to optimize each person's drive to define themselves uniquely in their environment. Self-actualization requires a culture of diversity.
4. No one is normal or average, everyone is a little bit weird, and we like that.

Yes, wise people around the world and throughout history have always known that helping others is the best way to build a strong, happy self. In the last forty years, it has become increasingly obvious that seeing the world this way may be the only way to be employable. You can't just go to school and get a job; you have to be valuable by being creative and being the kind of person others will want to work with.

In learning communities, people act as if this wisdom is already budding in children at birth ready to burst into full flower every day given the right conditions. Across the country, many young people today are increasingly aware that school is a waste of their time, and cast around for something worth doing. In their desperate flailing to matter, sometimes they can even be destructive.

Ask most kindergartners what they are looking forward to in school and they will say, "Friends." To be an education, school really must be in the friendship business, because this is the hardest and most important stuff—and the kids know it. Teachers know that maximizing individual success requires intense social engagement. Recess, cooperative learning groups, and practice at turning conflict into friendship are central to academic achievement.

We were wired by natural selection to make it in the world by partnering up with other humans, forming teams and organizing. Humans who tried to go it alone starved, got eaten by the tiger, or bludgeoned by "those-other-people-over-there." Our only hope was to stick together, and therefore, learning how to work things out with others was our main vehicle for getting smart. It still is.

"You wouldn't understand. You're white."
"Just because I'm white doesn't mean I don't understand."

The two people who spoke these words were fourteen, thirty-one years ago. They were eighth graders at my school in Oakland, California, when the Rodney King verdict came down.

I was going through old documents, lately, and saw my article that the *Montclarion* had published in May of 1992. When I read the article again, I got a burst of hope. Yes, the racism that has laced our country from its inception is still with us, and yet, when I zoom out and look at where we have come since 1992, I know the future will be brighter. Yes, it may have to get worse before it gets better, but the younger generation won't stand for it.

On April 30, 1992, our educational philosophy, our theories, our strategy were put to the test as the ugliness of the real world came home to our school in a way that was far more serious than the October fire in our backyard that fall. Not only had many of our students witnessed on TV the horror of extraordinary violence, murder, and chaos, but the older students from different racial and socioeconomic backgrounds were confronted with what they saw as an unbelievable miscarriage of justice, an injustice which shook their trust in our nation. Their feelings of insecurity, hurt and outrage came to visit our school on Thursday morning, April 30, 1992.

It was one of the proudest moments of my educational career, partly because we were ready. I gave no instructions to the faculty. We needed no meeting or assembly beforehand to address the issues. I simply clipped the appropriate articles from my two morning papers and went to school. I put the articles in the appropriate teachers' boxes and went back home to help get my children ready for school.

When I returned, several teachers and many students were standing out in front as usual. But this time the older ones were already talking about the verdict that exonerated four policemen of beating a motorist fifty-six times for over a minute.

I told Karen Ginsberg, Nicole Bessalo, and Lee Davis and that I had put the articles in their boxes in case they needed them. The middle-school teachers quickly reorganized, revising their schedules to discuss what was on everyone's mind. The two seventh grades met together for an hour-and-a-half lesson that they had prepared on the spur of the moment. The eighth graders did the same.

I was blessed to observe as thirty-two fourteen-year-olds (fifteen white, thirteen black, four Asian) sat in the circle with their social studies and English teachers and read the articles that had been distributed. The class made a list of all the facts they could glean from the articles, and then the discussion began.

The students discussed our system of justice and law enforcement: theory and practice, violence and counter-violence, racism, poverty, urban problems, disempowerment, alienation. Here's what our eighth graders were saying to each other.

"The governor of California just declared a state of emergency. I think that the state of emergency has been going on for two-hundred years."

"Of course, racism was the cause of the injustice. Do you really think the same thing would have happened if four black policemen had beaten a white man like that?"

"Well, I don't see how twelve jurors could have all been racists; both attorneys had to agree on all twelve."

(teacher) "If you were the attorney for Rodney King, what questions would you ask to determine if a prospective juror were a racist?"

The discussion was not merely academic. The students were talking about personal issues, too. And another source of pride for me was the harmony between our formal and informal (read real) curriculum.

"Sure, if I'd been there I'd have dragged that white man from the car and beaten him, too."

"Really? You think that kind of violence is justified?"

"Can any violence be justified?"

"You wouldn't understand. You're white."

"Just because I'm white doesn't mean I don't understand."

"Blacks aren't the only ones shocked by what happened; I'm white, and I agree with you."

"Yeah, but it's different."

"No, it's just the same."

"Yes, Race is a factor in my relationships. I am not as close to you as I thought I was because our skins are different colors"

"but it's not fair."

The national issues were personal issues. The students spoke from the heart; they spoke earnestly; they said hard things to each other; they listened; they expressed their feelings clearly; they constructed their arguments thoughtfully; they responded to each other in a disciplined way. The community held.

There were times when boundaries of civility were crossed, but in the end, the mutual respect that normally characterized their relationships held.

There seemed to be a sorrowful, profound sense that we are all in this together, and that the horrors outside can happen inside, if we are not careful, disciplined, responsible, compassionate, just, steadfast, sober, and prepared.

It was an hour-and-a-half of shared feelings, arguing, and confronting. This was not mere textbook learning. This was learning about democracy-in-action, not only "out there," but in ways that touched us where we live.

Of course, they acquired more of those skills and knowledge necessary for full participation in American democracy, but more deeply, they lost a little of their innocence.

There was no closure—how could there be? The students found their own closure *pro tem* by writing for the last ten minutes and then sharing what they wrote, if they chose.

I was happy that we had taken one more step down the long road toward mutual understanding between black and white and those with whom we differ, but I was proudest of the students. They revealed that they had met our highest educational objectives. I went to graduation with the knowledge that we were matriculating thirty-two young men and women of character, who will make a positive difference in the world.

It was also clear, that here, in the United States, regardless of our opinions about race, our biases, or ideology, our politics, we are all caught up in it.

When I hear on the news the horrors of the reality that our country is still laced with the racism that it was born with, it breaks my heart.

That one step that a few dozen eighth graders took twenty-seven years ago was no small step, and yet, I am discouraged at how poorly some of our leaders are at dealing with difference. Are we just marking time on the road to freedom?

But then I zoom out and do the math. I see that St. Paul's has been graduating about forty students like these for the last thirty-two years. There are several thousand schools that have been doing the same thing for a generation. They keep graduating more and more young people of all races who are good at turning conflict into mutual learning. These several million young people can be counted on to thwart racism wherever it rears its ugly head. By now they have had a positive influence on, maybe, a hundred people each. As they do, they continue to hone their skills. So, we are talking, maybe, tens of millions of adults who are somewhat skilled at a racially diverse democracy, and whose heads are not in the sand. That is not nothing.

Trump has brought the racists out of the closet, and increasingly, we can see this behavior for what it really is: a rearguard action of an obsolescent culture.

Children are windows into the human soul.

CHAPTER 25

Authority that Brings out the Authority in Others

When the best leader's work is done the people say, "We did it ourselves!"

—Lao Tse

Management-Speak Disguises a Dysfunctional Vision of School. On the surface much of the lingo of school improvement seems full of confident commitment to excellence and success for all. Language like accountability for measurable outcomes, high standards, data-driven decision-making, racing to the top, leaving no children behind, and so on, is seductive. Hearing this language in a school system one imagines thousands of children working hard to produce results that will someday make thousands of adults proud of their collective commitment to success.

But years of work based on these assumptions, and the vision does not materialize. Look at the data that data-driven managers keep collecting from the workers. Are we getting those "results?" If one were as rigorous as those words "data" and "accountability" pretend to be, one might conclude—or at least hypothesize—that our approach is wrong.

It is.

Education is leadership. Management kills learning. Children don't learn best when their growth is being managed. No one does. Compare the behaviors that result from management speak with the behaviors one sees in Gretchen's first-grade class.

Gretchen, a teacher in a Midwest school, treats her students as scientists. When they study penguins, for instance, they take expeditions to Antarctica as researchers. Each group of scientists is challenged to travel by boat, disembark, camp, observe conditions and penguins, record findings, return home, and present results. Students are measuring height, depth, temperature, decoding nautical signal flag messages, weighing, keeping a log, observing, and tallying penguin behaviors or playing math games on board ship to pass the time. One day some children slip into oversized black T-shirts to become their studied penguins, flapping flippers, collecting rocks, or huddling together. Other children use binoculars from icebergs across the room to tally observed behaviors. When the scientists return home they graph the results and present to the class.

I visit the class at story time and see twenty-four faces fixed on Gretchen in rapt attention as she reads a story related to their recent experiences. At the end of the unit, the students present their adventures and discoveries to older classes and to parents on Antarctica Day.

Gretchen's students take responsibility for their own learning because they own it; they feel that their teacher is trying to give them opportunities to shine.

Learning the conventions of academics in this context, their performance on standardized tests skyrockets right along with self-worth. We all learn better when we take on challenges that are meaningful to us.

A CHILD "CHALLENGED" IN THE MOMENT IS SEEN AS "AT RISK" AT SOME POINT THE FUTURE.

Management-speak hides a fear of long-term consequences that distracts from the real work of education. This, paradoxically, results in shortsighted action. Lessons become tests of worthiness, indicators of which students are likely to make it and which are at risk. A child "challenged" in the moment is seen as "at risk" at some point in the future. Teachers are held accountable for "covering the material" toward some vision of future success.

But this vision is a mirage, of course. Making kindergarten more academic does not result in better academic performance by fourth grade. Play is important for optimal brain development—that's why kids take to it. The results of this development are so multifaceted, complex, and interdependent that you can't measure the academic results with any validity or reliability.

By contrast, Gretchen's students live in the present, thus preparing them for a future of enthusiastic learning. Focusing on children's natural love of learning in the moment builds a love of challenge, resilience through failure and better long-term results. Measuring-up clouds may hover over Gretchen's head, but there is no mirage of success on the horizon. She and her students are exploring the planet not trudging through an empty desert.

Gretchen acted as if she knew that she was leading a group of natural-born scientists and made sure they got lots of experience and training in the disciplines of being scientists. One day I asked what her secret was. She said, "Do the present right, and the future will take care of itself."

No one is at fault that education is not happening in most school systems. Systems tend to be insensitive to the active ingredients of education: internal motivation, individual decision-making, unique characters, directly observable data, and love.

Many people could, however, take responsibility. System leaders could hold teachers accountable for what really matters. Teachers could be true to their calling. We, the people, could expect educators to educate rather than simply follow directions and sort children into categories.

It may seem like a management nightmare but that is the leadership challenge.

CHAPTER 26

Teacher Authority, Boundaries, and the Business of School

Creativity requires the courage to let go of certainties.

—Erich Fromm

Sitting in the speaker's chair at morning meeting Claire presented a yellow silk scarf to her class. As she spoke, she floated it through her hands and around her neck, all eyes of her second-grade classmates were on her.

When she was finished talking, she asked: "Does anyone have a question?" and when six hands went up she hesitated, looking at each one before calling on James, who asked, "Did you ever think of using it in a dance?"

For ten minutes the questions kept coming. Ginny, the teacher, was particularly happy when she heard "Why do you think it's so expensive?" because she saw an opportunity to make a connection to the study of silkworms she was planning for the afternoon.

Claire spoke quietly but with authority and everyone listened. It felt good to be someone who knew something that interested others. With each question Claire's authority grew, and her way encouraged the inquiry of others.

I was reminded of this moment during a conversation with John, a photographer in his thirties and my seatmate on a flight from New York to Chicago two months ago.

Our conversation about education took a turn for the deeper when John said, "The core problem with education today is authority. These days, students don't respect teacher authority. Students tune them out and turn to some other source of knowledge."

We all have the same the image in our head when we hear that statement: a generic high school teacher trying to lead a generic class of adolescents who could care less. The image springs, if not from our own experience, then from watching "Ferris Bueller's Day Off," or any number of movies with scenes from high school.

My daughter, the professor of political theory at Vanderbilt, feels this lack of automatic authority, herself. She is well aware that she is competing for her students' attention. She's concerned that her students might be on their smart phones while she is teaching, but she takes it as a challenge rather than an insult.

There are those who blame "the parents" for the fact that "kids don't respect authority" anymore. But before we jump at scapegoats, there are some questions it would be wise to ask, questions like: What is authority today? Where does it come from? As our world changes could teachers and schools stay the same?

In talking with John about these questions, Claire's authority and the way Claire's teacher envisioned her job came to mind and made me ask: "If someone talks and no one listens, does he have authority?"

Obviously, it's a rhetorical question with one answer: of course not. You are no leader if you have no followers. The relationship between author and audience is symbiotic. Authority is not simply based on knowing stuff; it is based on knowing stuff that is of interest and benefit to others–as they define "benefit." A teacher's attempt to input knowledge outside the context of a student's sense of purpose is my idea of a waste of time.

A generation after teacher authority based on position was replaced by authority based on knowledge, authority based on knowledge is also risk. Today, by the time children are thirteen they know that there are many ways to acquire knowledge (Google, Wikipedia, YouTube, and Texting to name a few), and teachers are usually "not your best source."

If knowledge can be gained easily without going to school, what is the point of school? This question is analogous to what railroad people should have asked themselves as soon as the first airplane took passengers from New York to Chicago. Is transporting people around the country the highest and best use of a railroad?

Residents of St. Louis should have asked such a question as soon as they heard of a railroad track being built down the Mississippi on the other side. Is getting goods and people to New Orleans the highest and best use of a riverboat?

These questions were asked too late. If the acquisition of knowledge is not the highest and best use of school, then what is? Perhaps a school is a vehicle for bringing people together for the purpose of growing their authority. If so, then, what's the highest and best use of a teacher?

Claire's authority is built on her ability to increase the authority of her classmates. Ginny's authority is based on her ability to organize activities that will give her students opportunities to grow their authority.

If building authority in others is the business of education, then there are radical implications for the training of teachers and the reorganization of schools.

Authority and Boundaries

It's 5:15 pm. Mom is at the stove making dinner. Her six-year-old Brittany sees a bag of candy canes that her mother just brought home for Christmas decorations, and says, "Mommy, can I have a candy cane?"

"It's close to dinnertime. Can you wait?"

"No. I'm hungry," says Brittany with a bit of a whine in her voice.

"We'll be eating soon. I don't want you to spoil your dinner."

"But I'm hungry. I can't wait," Brittany complains.

Silence.

"Mommy. I want a candy cane. I'm hungry." Brittany's tone has changed to a wail.

Long pause. "Okay, but just one," with a resigned tone of voice that communicates "I don't really think it's a good idea, but if that is what you want, then okay, you win."

This kind of back-and-forth between parent and child can often last quite a bit longer and is rather common in American households. Boundaries in American families are often rather vague and poorly defended with results ranging from authority battles at home, to misbehavior in public, to discipline problems at school—even to sloppy parent-teacher conferences.

Americans are all over the map on authority. From authoritarians to anti-authoritarians and everything in between, we have among us many notions of authority, mostly negative. So, we tend to avoid the word.

But we need the word. Children need us to be authorities. They are counting on us to be authorities on nutrition, our own personal boundaries, how we treat one another, and thousands of other bits of knowledge about how the world works. Moreover, we want children to *become* authorities—that's why we send them to school. We want them to be authors, authors of books, articles, poems, works of art, new inventions, new companies, better ways of doing things. We need them to be authors of peace and friendship.

Setting Boundaries Supports Young Decision-Makers

Fifteen years ago, as I was driving north with Lizzie, my nineteen-year-old daughter, she said: "Dad, you never gave me the No Smoking Lecture."

"I know," I replied. "I always trusted you."

"But I needed it."

"What do you mean, you needed it?"

"You do know I smoked, right?"

"No. Well, I guess I remember Mom finding a pack of cigarettes in your room, but I wasn't worried about it."

"Why not?"

"As I said, I have always trusted your decision-making abilities."

"Well, you should have. I needed the No Smoking Lecture."

"Really? Why? Are you addicted?"

"No, but I needed it."

"Okay I am sorry I didn't give it to you."

"No, Dad. I still need it. I want the No Smoking Lecture. Now."

"Okay Don't smoke," I said off handedly.

"That's not the No Smoking Lecture!"

"But I don't do the No Smoking Lecture. I don't even know the No Smoking Lecture."

"Certainly, you know the No Smoking Lecture. It begins with 'Listen, Kid. Smoking is a dirty, filthy habit. . .' and then goes on from there."

"Okay" (I pulled over to the side of the road and stopped because to do it properly, of course, I had to look her straight in the eyes.) "Listen. Smoking is a dirty, filthy habit. It is unattractive. It makes your breath smell bad, and it marks you as a certain kind of person—a kind of person I don't like, and I don't want you to be or look like that kind of person. A girl who smoked could never be my girlfriend, and I would certainly never marry one. Smoke will do damage to a fetus in your womb; it will give you cancer and a variety of other serious diseases. In fact, smoking can kill you. I do not want you to smoke. Do you understand?"

"Yes, Dad. I understand."

"Good." Then added, "How did I do?"

"That was great, Dad. Thank you."

Why did she want me to give her the No Smoking Lecture? I don't know. I should have asked her. Did she feel "under-parented?" Had I under-communicating my values. By trusting her was I communicating I didn't care? I was always impressed with her and her values and her good behavior. By thinking she was a good decision-maker, was I forgetting that all kids need to know where we stand on things—even after they have gone off to college?

Apparently, just because we trust our children doesn't mean we can't lecture them. They need to hear where we stand; it is useful information for any young decision-maker, even if they have already proven themselves to be good decision-makers.

Recent brain research shows what we have always known about adolescents: they are way too open-minded. They have heard, for instance, that you shouldn't smoke, but their friends do, and . . . This is why teenagers do crazy things. They seem to have to find out for themselves. But to learn firsthand that you will die from smoking is a lifelong project that I wouldn't want Lizzie to undertake.

Just because we define and clarify boundaries to them does not mean we don't trust them. On the contrary, we are implying that we know that they will make their own decisions; we just want to give them the benefit of our experience. If they have our voice in their head telling them that smoking is bad (or whatever) at least when they are reckless, they will be reckless a little more carefully.

If, however, our lecture is an attempt to control our teen's behavior, we are going to make things a lot more difficult. By the time they are thirteen, we are playing the game of high responsibility/low control. We have to treat them as if they know what they are doing, even though we know that they don't, quite. It can be a little scary. This apparently paradoxical dance can drive people (parents and children alike) crazy unless the parent understands that taking responsibility for a child does not mean controlling them. Raising children is an exercise in learning from mistakes.

Bottom line: we don't have to do everything right, and we don't have to think of everything. If we pay attention and listen to our children, they will show us or tell us what they need, and we will be able to talk with them about it.

The Authority of Teachers

Authority is a good word. Teachers are charged with making sure that their students leave them more authoritative than they were before. All good teachers want their students to be writers regardless of subject, because getting their children to write about what they are learning is a very helpful way to solidify the thoughts and understandings that will make them authorities. Speaking in front of a group is a critical activity if children are to become the strong social animals they need to be for optimal functioning in the world—right up there with reading, writing, and ciphering.

That these obvious statements are so often in the shadows of our minds rather than the forefront is partial proof of my thesis that we are authority-avoidant even though authority-avoidance is about as functional as conflict avoidance.

Vicky is at the keyboard trying to concentrate on her writing. Beatty, her six-year-old, comes into the room talking. "Mommy, . . ." he says, and the contents of his mind come pouring out.

Vicky stops typing, turns to him, listens and answers his questions even though she is feeling a lot of deadline pressure.

For her own sake as well as for the child's, a much better move would be to say in a matter-of-fact voice, "Please don't walk into a room talking." Or perhaps, "Wait, please. I need to finish my thought."

At the crux of the matter is the reality that any two people working on their own individual authority are different; so their authorities may clash. How will my authority run afoul of some other person's authority? What if we disagree? Who will win? Who will show me up as less than the authority I think I am?

One of the disciplines required for handling clashes of authority is defining and defending boundaries. Being clear about what you think, feel, want, need, and value is actually a gift rather than an imposition. People need to know where they stand with us in order to build a relationship. Kids in particular appreciate it (even if they sometimes sound like they don't.)

To maximize education, a school or home must organize itself so that each person's authority enhances other people's authority. Defining ourselves clearly and lovingly to children is a critical discipline that takes a lot of practice—in fact, it is a lifelong challenge, but it is at the core of building authority in children.

Brittany's and Beatty's mothers are doing more than being wishy-washy about boundaries. They are missing opportunities to challenge their children to become more flexible, resilient, adaptable, and creative. Frustrating a child's impulse is essential for his success in all endeavors from social problems to math problems.

CHAPTER 27

Authority, Imperfection, and Behavior Problems

Genius is the recovery of childhood at will.

—Arthur Rimbaud

One day Iliana (age six) seemed to want to strike up a conversation as she was leaving school with her Mom.

"Goodbye, Mr. Rick."

"Goodbye, Iliana."

"You're the principal."

"That's right. I am the principal."

"You are in charge of everything."

"That's right."

"You can DO anything you want."

At that point I realized I was in a different conversation—not the usual pleasantries in which mutual affection is communicated but a conversation with substance.

"Well, no, Iliana, I can't do anything I want. I have to obey the same rules you do. I have to respect everyone. I have to be kind all the time."

"Yeah, you have to follow the rules on the play structure."

"Right," I said. Then a little thought: "Actually, *you* can do some things I can't do. I can't climb on the play structure. I am too big."

I miss having children around. Their absence compromises my education.

If you are lucky enough to be responsible for the education of children but are not feeling so lucky right now (like they test your authority too much, or ask too many questions, or keep getting into conflict, or keep making mistakes, or their achievement is sub-par, or in some other way just too challenging), maybe it would be more relaxing to frame the challenge differently.

Maybe *they* are doing *their* job (learning how to make something of themselves in the world), and *you* need to let *them* help *you* with *your* job (learning how to make something of *yourself* in the world). Here are some little mantra-type things we can keep in mind.

1. *Challenging authority?*—Play position. Their job *is* to test the environment. Your job is to *be there*, pushing back when necessary. They are working at becoming an authority, themselves.
2. *Asking too many questions?*—Their job is questioning; yours is answering. (. . .and sometimes with a question of your own.)
3. *Getting into conflict?*—Good. They have learning opportunities. (We might have an opportunity to help make it a learning experience . . . or not)
4. *Making mistakes?* Mistakes are learning opportunities. Their job is to create. Yours is to deliver feedback that is hearable, seeable, and doable (sometimes).
5. *Achievement is too low?*—Loving the challenge of learning IS the achievement. ("Achievement" is a by-product and often a function of luck.)

Life provides us all with the same fundamental challenge: the challenge of learning the art of allowing ourselves to be changed. As Carol Dweck keeps reminding us, success depends on maintaining a growth mindset.[1] Adults can help by counteracting our brains' natural affinity for fixed mindsets.

CHAPTER 28

True Authority Leaves Room for Others to Exercise Their Authority

Nothing strengthens authority so much as silence.

—Leonardo da Vinci

Recently, at the West Hollywood Library in the children's room, I witnessed a real pro in charge of seven two-year-olds. What I observed was a model of education as leadership, leadership that created the conditions for the children to exercise their own decision-making capabilities—their own leadership.

This young woman just sat, watched, and reacted. The children generated all the action: touching, testing, choosing, initiating, proposing, exploring, fitting and not fitting, building and knocking down, trying, failing, trying again, taking, talking, disagreeing, defending, agreeing, following, conflicting, and resolving their own conflicts without adult intervention. Watching all this humanity in motion was magical.

From time to time the adult corrected bad behavior. Leaving little room for confusion about what was okay and what was not. She rarely used her emotions as messages. The children did a lot of self-correcting.

Her power seemed to emanate from her unflappableness. Her calm, uneffusive presence was, itself, a message: "This is the way one wants to be." She seemed to see her job as presider, the authority on the throne, the ground of their being. The kids were the show, not her. Her role was guardian and guide.

We hear a lot about the virtue of "consistency" with children. What was consistent was her affect: business like—almost deadpan. She reacted honestly and straightforwardly to everything. The children always knew where they stood with her. They were not, however, always able to predict her response.

Some misbehavior seemed an important part of the learning experience—finding out where this paragon of adult integrity and reliability stood on things. It's as if the thought in a toddler's head was: "I know I am not supposed to grab something someone else is playing with, but this is a slightly different situation. I wonder how the law applies in this case."

Other misbehaviors seemed to have the purpose of checking in—checking for a reaction from time to time to see if the queen was still on the throne, still standing for what she has always stood for.

When her session in the library was over, I talked to her. I had to find out who this person was. It turns out she is a babysitter.

Creating Environments for Children to Do Their Social Experiments

These same phenomena can be seen at all ages. Judy Stone, one of the all-time great middle school teachers, and I were in charge of forty-eight seventh and eighth graders for their forty-five-minute lunch/recess period one rainy day in March several years ago. We were in an old parish hall that had not yet been fitted out for children. Judy called us all together at the beginning and said: "There are three rules: no running, no throwing balls, and no jumping off the stage."

CHILDREN ARE SCIENTISTS
WHOSE MAIN FIELD OF RESEARCH IS SOCIAL DYNAMICS.

For forty-five minutes there was no bad behavior. However, Judy did spend the rest of her time adjudicating whether or not what we had just observed was "running" or a fast walk, "jumping" or a giant step. Was that projectile that went flying past us a "ball" or a wad of duct tape? Now and then we had a student take a ten-minute timeout, but all fifty of us—the thirteen- and fourteen-year-olds and the two fifty-year-olds alike—had a good time together even though the constraints and restrictions of our environment were somewhat unusual and cruel for active children.

Contrary to popular opinion, children are not fundamentally selfish, brutish barbarians naturally bent on chaos needing to be taught right from wrong. Humans are naturally social beings whose brains are designed to make something of themselves and that includes learning the ways of collaboration. Research by Alison Gopnik, Patricia Kuhl, and others shows that children in the first five years of life utilize the scientific method all day long, that their central research question is what causes what, and that their main field of research is social dynamics (New York, 2010).

What did Judy and the babysitter have in common? What did they do right? They saw their children as scientists and that the design of the laboratories they created would teach what their children needed to learn. Like the stereotypical London bobby, they were a presence. They acted as if they trusted the inner voices of children to guide them in mostly good directions—that the directions they were going in at least had some legitimate motive. They acted as if that they could count on their children to self-direct, solve problems, collaborate, communicate, learn to control themselves, and contribute.

But this does not mean being wishy-washy. On the contrary, it requires that we be centered on our commitment to kindness, fairness, beauty, truth, love, and justice. In the laboratory, we create, children need to see us standing up for the world our souls want to see.

What did we do right?

1) Our attitude: "These are all good kids and we know it will be hard for them to live within the restrictions this environment is putting on them." Unspoken but assumed. We understood their "misbehavior" as their need to understand the meaning and the reality of the boundaries.
2) Real boundaries: The rules represented actual requirements of the environment rather than something derived mysteriously from adult willpower. The boundaries were not a choice but a necessity, like driving on the right side of the road.—We didn't explain.
3) No punishment: Consequences were just that. "If you go beyond the pale; you will take a breather until you can show us you are ready to be a responsible member of society."—unspoken but assumed.
4) Nothing else: That's all there was to it. Questions of authority, respect, discipline, good-and-bad did not enter in, because they acted as if these were not in question. They did not waste breath (and credibility) explaining things that they wanted them to take for granted. They treated them as wise (as in "a word to the wise is sufficient.")

Defending Boundaries

One summer evening Max found himself supervising his three-year-old niece Sara as she swam in her grandparents' pool, the rest of the adults having gone in to make dinner. At six o'clock the call came from the kitchen: "Time for diiiiin-ner!"

"Okay, Sara," he said. "Time for dinner."

Sara ignored him. She continued paddling by the edge of the pool not four feet from him with no change in behavior. She didn't even look at him. When he could see that she could hear because her head was out of the water, he said: "Let's go, Sara. They called us to dinner" and got no reaction.

Ignoring someone is rude, and being ignored feels bad. With some annoyance in his voice he said: "Come on, Sara. Time to get out."

Again, faced with no reaction he said: "Sara, it is time for dinner. If you don't get out by the time I count to three, I will get you out." No reaction.

"One" got no reaction.

"Two" still got no reaction, but at what would have been "Two-and-a-half" she gave him a glance.

At "Three" he reached into the pool and pulled her out.

She stood there by the side of the pool dripping wet saying: "I hate you. I hate you. I hate you." Then, she stomped ahead of Max up the hill to dinner.

It hurt. No one likes to hear "I hate you" from someone they love. But since that day he and Sara have had a great relationship—friendly, loving, and respectful.

Though not necessarily a model of good parenting, his behavior was simple, straightforward, and human. She ignored him. It made him mad. He made her get out of the pool and insisted on his prerogatives as the person responsible for her. She communicated the simple truth. Making her stop swimming made her mad.

A natural first reaction to "I hate you" might be self-doubt, guilt, or indecision. A good adult response to a childish "I hate you" might simply be to acknowledge her feelings. If he had said back to Sara: "I hear that you are angry. I understand," he would have been translating his empathy for her disappointment into words without letting her outburst change his decision. A longer version might have been: "I know you are mad at me. I am sorry you feel that way, but you left me no choice. We simply have to go to dinner." Talking like this to children not only helps you stay on track, but also builds their social-emotional intelligence by showing them how to put words to feelings.

At the same time, having this kind of presence of mind is also not necessary for raising responsible, respectful children. We might not be smart enough to think of these words on the spot, but kids are smart enough to get the idea. Furthermore, too many words and children will pick up that we are trying to convince ourselves of something we are actually ambivalent about. What was critical for Max was sticking to his guns in his own less-than-perfect way. That was something she could respect—and did.

It is natural for parents to hate it when their kids get mad, or cry, or are otherwise emotionally upset, but it is important for us to steel ourselves against it, so that we respond rather than react. If you find not reacting challenging (and most of us do), here are some mantras you can write on Post-it's on your bathroom mirror:

1. Under-react.
2. Keep your adult neediness to yourself.
3. Over-explaining undermines your authority.
4. Don't lecture on something that could be assumed.

Children count on adults to be authorities. They are counting on parents to decide what is right and to insist on it without compromise or apology. When we back-peddle, pull a punch, or act uncertain, we cause confusion and make trouble for our children and for ourselves as well. If the truth is that we are uncertain, that's okay. Just say so.

Kids just want to know where we stand. It is critical data for them to become good decision-makers themselves.

AN AUTHORITY VACUUM MAKES PEOPLE ANXIOUS AND ANXIOUS PEOPLE GENERALLY BEHAVE BADLY.

Yes, children want to make their own decisions and become authorities themselves, but they do not want to do this in an authority vacuum. In Sara's case, her parents had recently gotten divorced, and she was looking for some adult to exercise adult authority. Children like knowing that their social world is not a chaotic free-for-all. An authority vacuum makes people anxious and anxious people generally behave badly.

How should we "Let them know who's boss?" How should we exercise authority with grace? Maybe Max wishes he had found a more graceful way, but at least he did define a boundary. He defined himself, and she understood that he was an authority she could count on. At least, he was worthy of respect because the decisions he made came from his core—the origin of his authority. Sara knew all this and that was sufficient. The good news is we don't have to be perfect.

For best results, if schools aspire to be the kinds of learning communities that maximize student potential, all the educators have to be this kind of leader.

Isn't the job of a teacher to increase the students' abilities as authors, researchers, problem-solvers, decision makers? To pull this off we can't be afraid of the word authority. Teachers, of course, need to be authorities and need to be good at exercising this authority in ways that increase the students' authority.

Whether we are a school principal or a teacher or just a uncle supervising your niece, everyone is counting on us to be true to ourselves, and we should be ready to do what our integrity requires regardless of the consequences because the worst consequence is not death, but the violation of our integrity.

Part of increasing the ability of teachers to exercise of this kind of authority is a principal's ability to define and defend boundaries. If doubt arises about the defense of boundaries, it undermines all legitimate authority. Adults as well as kids want to know that there is someone in charge who will keep them on the right path and out of harm's way. This tendency to test where our limits are with other people, doesn't stop. Most adults are still testing where their authority rubs up against someone else's authority.

Therefore, we should always be ready to fall back on beginning a sentence with "My integrity requires . . ." Or "I cannot in good conscience . . ." This may not make the other person happy, but, it's hard to argue with. And at least we are telling the truth.

Behavior Problems Rooted in Kids' Scientific Brains

What underlies "bad behavior?"

Several years ago, I would meet three other adults from time to time at a preschool to go for a walk with some four-year-olds. In the classroom, the teacher invites eight children to pick a partner.

"This is Mr. Rick," says the teacher. "Who wants to walk with Mr. Rick?"

Samuel immediately comes over to this perfect stranger and takes my hand. Renee scrutinizes my face, gives me a beguiling look, and pushes past two others to take my hand.

We walk out of the classroom, down the hall, out the door, and through the parking lot. After stopping at a street and looking both ways, we cross to the sidewalk on the other side.

We examine different kinds of nuts on the ground and never miss honoring each puddle with our feet in some creative way. But most of the fun comes from the constant chatter. I am proud that I am able to keep up two conversations at once–sort of.

Two-thirds of the way through the walk Renee decides it is time to take our relationship to the next level. She drops my hand. The adult behind me says: "Hold hands, Renee," and Renee retakes my hand.

But her experimenting has only just begun. At a curb she finds an excuse to drop it, again. Renee spends the last ten minutes of the walk doing research on our relationship by trying out a repertoire of behaviors. It seems she has a list of questions she needs to get more data on:

Does Mr. Rick uphold the "hold hands" rule?

If he does, how does his way differ from the other adults who have held my hand on this walk before?

How does Mr. Rick assert his authority? About what? Are other rules more or less important than hand-holding?

I am pretty confident these are some of her questions, and I am sure she has some other hypotheses she is also testing, but what can you tell in a thirty-minute walk?

I have been reading many wise statements online about behavior problems and their causes: "She needs attention," "product of laissez-fair parenting," "Mother is a control freak," "the evils of over-protection," and many more you could guess. However, there is a very common cause that I rarely hear much about. Much childish behavior that adults feel is bad is the result of a routine scientific investigation of the environment. Testing hypotheses like: "Whining gets me what I want." Always? No matter who is in charge? Who has more authority, Mom, Dad, Grandma, baby sitter? . . . or Mr. Rick? . . . on and on.

Does this adult mean what he says? Does he handle the same situation in the same way as another? Does "No eating between meals" mean the same thing to different adults. When a teacher says, "No running," does he mean "No fast walking?"

Children absolutely need to know the answers to these and thousands of questions like them. In my experience, that is the primary cause of what we adults call misbehavior.

All four-year-old's have been doing research on their environment for thirty-five thousand hours, and the largest area of interest for most children is social relationships, how people behave, and how you can get them to behave. By the time she walks in the door of a kindergarten next year Renee will have had plenty of practice harmonizing her needs, values, and interests with those of others. It's a crime to waste her time, a crime that she feels as disrespect.

We humans acquired our large brains, because one branch of the primate line started to get serious about collaborating. There is good research to supporting the hypothesis that our large brains are a result of developing the sophisticated language necessary for solving all sorts of social problems from passing on knowledge of how to make new things to resolving conflict to building culture. Research by Alison Gopnik, Patricia Kuhl, and others shows that children in the first five years of life have built their brains into causal maps of the world and especially ways they can impact it.[1]

Children's social competence includes an understanding of authority relationships. For them to live a successful life and us to live a happy life with them, we need to design this causal map so that it includes a sophisticated notion of authority based on the foundation that the measure of a person's authority is their ability to increase the authority of others. Doing this requires a set of disciplines that, for best results, we have been practicing all along.

1. Defining your point of integrity.
2. Respecting others as self-actualizers.
3. Play the Collaborate, Create, Contribute Game.
4. Listen with a willingness to learn.
5. Dodge authority battles by surprise, humor, and changing the context.

(These disciplines become easier if we have a good relationship with our genius.)

CHAPTER 29

Integrity: Bringing Your Whole Self to the Table

We have all a better guide in ourselves, if we would attend to it, than any other person can be.

—Jane Austen

The design flaws in *Homo sapiens* have a saving grace.

One morning in February 1986, I awoke from a dream and said out loud: "I said that???!!!" I was horrified. While I slept my brain had replayed a moment from five months ago, an experience that had escaped my notice at the time but had terrible meaning for me, now.

It remembered "Back to School Night" at Cathedral School. I was at the podium in front of a couple hundred parents and teachers, welcoming them to a brand-new school year. At the end of my keynote remarks that set the tone for the year, I went through the schedule for the evening. It was a little complicated and so I finished with, "It will be a little like a Chinese fire drill, so please be patient. It will all work out, and you will get to see the classes you want to see."

"Chinese fire drill!" An ethnic slur! I can't believe I said that!

I was focusing on many other things, so I gave no thought to what I had said and forgot about it. The meeting ended and parents went to their children's classes. No one came up to me afterward to point out my *faux pas*.

Cathedral School prided itself on its racial and cultural diversity. I had made diversity the centerpiece of our educational philosophy. "Diversity is most fundamentally about making every aspect of the school culture support each person's unique, continuous self-definition," I would say. "A safe place to be yourself" was one of our slogans, and we were proud of it. Now we have the head of the school saying something about a "Chinese fire drill!" There were a dozen Chinese families in my audience! That I had made an ethnic slur in front of the entire school never really entered my consciousness. No one spoke to me about it that night. No one mentioned it the next day.

But I did finally get the message, not from another person, not from the community, but from my subconscious. My genius—always with my best interest at heart—picked four o'clock in the morning five months after the event as the time to educate me.

"Self" (as in "myself") is actually several selves. My self has an executive director. It plans, strategizes, makes decisions, tries to win, explains things, tries to understand, to make sense, and to keep everything under control. It's the self that answers the question, "What do you do?" when someone meets you. It knows how to cook, take care of others, clean up, draw pictures, make friends, and write—or not. It acquires, sorts, and categorizes information, can tell you the names of things, knows right from wrong, and is responsible for keeping ourselves in right relationship with others—and the whole world. This self is sometimes aware of a relationship self as well as an individual self.

Our executive director has an impossible job, though, mostly because it is responsible for a whole brain, of which it is mostly unaware. All those experiences I have forgotten or repressed, the data that came in when I was paying attention to something else, the stuff I didn't understand, my inadequacies—all this and so much that I can only guess at—comprise my unknown self. I like to think of myself as a caring, open-minded, inclusive soul that would never dream of insulting someone else. Oops.

The gift I was given at four in the morning forty years ago is the reminder that being a person of integrity is a never-ending process of trial and error. I keep trying to be the self I want to be, and each attempt is an opportunity to discover parts of me that still need to be integrated into who I am. I usually bring only "myself" to a situation and leave my other selves on the sidelines. Then, I find myself doing things I don't intend, forgetting to do things that I do intend, and getting reactions that I don't expect. I screw up. I fail. I make mistakes and enemies. Too late, I discover that I was wrong—or worse, avoid such discoveries altogether. In order to preserve the illusion of wholeness, I tend to forget the bad stuff and it becomes part of "not me."

Our executive self would rather not uncover this mess. Every experience we have—"good" or "bad"—is a new resource, but our executive self would just as soon not know about the bad. We would like to proceed through life as if on Facebook, from one prettiness to another, chalking up achievements, victories, and friends. How can I accomplish my goals plagued by all my inadequacies and vast quantities of data that don't fit with what I think I know and what I am trying to be? How can I keep it together? Making an ethnic slur is something *I* would never do.

The thought that I might do the very thing I abhor is enough to make me live in perpetual fear—fear that bad parts of me will be found out, or worse, fear that I am made of bad stuff, or worst, that my true self is bad. But the good news is that our unknown self is not actually so bad. The good news is that we have a character, that the gods imprinted this character on our soul at birth, that this character has a voice, that it is sending us messages all the time, and that we can partner-up with this voice and make decisions that express our whole selves. My executive self has a partner with a sense of humor—a jester.

With the help of this jester, acting with integrity is always a possibility, and the moments we create can be glorious. Our jester can help us make our many parts work in harmony. Trying to conquer or suppress these hidden selves is a formula for perpetuating the problem.

That voice that woke me up at 4 a.m. to tell me something—we all have it, and it is talking to us all the time. Leaders need to have a relationship with this voice. Are we listening? Where do these messages come from? I don't know, but I have learned that we must listen, respect, and honor them, because they are part of us. The more aware of them we are, and the more we learn to listen carefully, we will discover that they are on our side.

Anyway, they are a part of us whether we like it or not. I have discovered (as have many people) that we all have a muse.

Our genius knows us more than we know ourselves. It loves us more than we think we are loveable; it expresses itself in a wide variety of ways. When we are "playing out of our head," working with abandon, or "in the flow" barely conscious of what we are doing, when our various selves are in partnership, driven by love not fear, our executive self can let go and let our genius lead us.

Genius is playful, has a sense of humor, is creative, is not insensitive to the needs of others, but on the contrary, is passionate about them. Genius calls us to take responsibility, to act, to make decisions. Genius is devoted to Grace, Wisdom, Love, Truth, Justice, and Beauty and is a little oblivious as to social convention and moral codes. Young children are excellent windows into genius.

Furthermore, genius is a necessary guide to integrity, to being whole. In fairytales, it's the relative who doesn't get invited to the christening who becomes the evil witch. It's a basic truth about our psyches. Parts of ourselves that we deny, or devalue, or do not recognize will cause us trouble until we welcome them into ourselves. Integrating our various selves into one harmonious whole is a lifelong project; don't attempt it without consulting your genius.

The "evil witch" concept is also true in a group. Creating a more inclusive culture engenders more leadership behavior. In less inclusive cultures people who are not valued find ways of making a difference any way they can, and sometimes, those ways are not constructive; sometimes they are downright murderous and evil.

Yes. Reality and our trusted beliefs never quite match up. Other people are always a potential problem. Culture can be a nasty prison. But our soul holds the key to living with the confusion long enough for us to create something of value. Our genius is in league with the genius in others.

All artists know that executive self is incapable of producing beauty without our genius. Their total commitment to beauty sends a signal to genius—an invitation to bring genius to the table. The same is true for all of us. When Justice, Truth, Love and Grace are our metrics, we create a space for genius to show up and tell us what to do and what to say. Genius told Solomon to say, "Cut the baby in half." Genius told Rosa Parks to say, "I'm tired."

Organized religions are time-honored ways of accessing the spirit, but religion does not have a monopoly on spirituality. All of us have an inner teacher, and there are many ways to access it.

Bobby Richman, a close friend who used to write music for Sesame Street and now brings his music to senior centers, tells the following story:

Two elderly people moved clumsily and with difficulty down the nursing home hallway, one with the aid of a cane, and the other with walker. When they opened the door to my music classroom and heard African music with a brisk, snappy rhythm, they cast aside their walking aids, embraced and began to dance together with fervor and joy.

It's a critical concept when working with children, too. In school, where there is enthusiasm there is a divine spirit, also. *Enthousiasmos* means "imbued with the divine." What young children have going for them is that they *always* bring *all* of themselves to a situation, at least in the first six years of their lives. They have not yet separated their mind from their soul, their heart from their feet, their hands from their natural scientific approach to problems.

All joyful moments, successful partnerships, and peace of mind require harmony in the brain. When our spirit is in the game, we are "playing out of our head," "the scales fall away from our eyes," we can "see clearly," and our actions lead us toward Beauty, Truth, Justice and Love. Music activates the soul and integrates our heart, body, and mind so that we approach the world whole.

Likewise, so many of our failures and frustrations, and certainly, all the evils perpetrated by us and by others, come from partial engagement of the brain—a failure to bring our whole selves to a challenge. We are "dark as Erebus," when our aspirations, investigations, and pursuits are divorced from our spirit. Dissociated from our soul, our imagination is sidelined, our range of movement shrinks, and our relationships are at risk.

But music and dancing are by no means the only activators of the soul. Myths, poetry, art, theatre, jogging, scripture, rituals, prayer, meditation, and long walks are also time-tested practices. And like music and dancing, not all these practices are equal. "By their fruits ye shall know them." Bad art is the result of an executive brain out of touch with its muse. In fact, the quality of any art or spiritual practice is the degree to which it actually *does* liberate, express, and speak to the soul.

Genius is expert in harmonizing inconsistent opposites, resolving dilemmas, and integrating two impossibilities, and expressing what our integrity requires, and this can have a powerful impact on our social context. In fact, we owe it to ourselves, others, and society to have that impact, because our soul is not satisfied if our relationships are not right. We can make more moments like the those in this book by building our relationships with our genius.

We humans are each poor, sorry, weird creatures trying to become whole by making a difference to those around us. Let's not forget that this is the mission all children are on.

We each have a genius that is working the problem all the time. Each of us has opportunities every day to create the context in which we work and play. Enlisting the help of our genius in communicating, collaborating, creating, and contributing increases the likelihood that we will increase the quality of these critical human imperatives in our lives.

I have come to call this phenomenon "genius," but it goes by many names: spirit, muse, psyche, calling, soul, daemon, Geist, kami, wisdom, the voice of our character, the voice of a god, Lord, God, or Allah.

Today, in our culture, most of these words have taken on other meanings and genius is a good example. The original Roman meaning of genius, for example, is "the tutelary spirit of a person, place or institution." Until very recently this was the first meaning in English dictionaries. (*Oxford English* 1982). But genius has all but lost that meaning in today's culture. In our ability-ist culture it has come to mean "an unusual gift, talent or intelligence," and that distracts us from a more valuable use of the word. Other words for this voice have acquired a vast array of other distractions. Only the German "Geist" has not drifted far from the original concept of spirit-with-agency, as in Zeitgeist, "the spirit of the times."

For us to create educational cultures that keep humanity from becoming extinct, we must keep returning to that voice that calls us toward our character, our calling, the difference we are supposed to make in the world, the voice that expresses our integrity and integrates us with all the disparate elements in challenging moments.

Scientists might call this geistly phenomenon a "para phenomenon," by which they would mean that there is "no scientific evidence for it. Based on the body of knowledge that has so far been empirically verified, it does not exist." But to mark a phenomenon as "para" does not mean it is not a phenomenon. To say that soul or genius or calling or Geist does not exist is to ignore a vast body of human experience going back at least to the dawn of history. Every culture at every age has had a name for it, and there is a vast body of spiritual practices that people have come up with to access this genius. The three ghosts who visited Scrooge in his dreams came from the same place—deep inside. If we don't listen to our genius during the day, it speaks to us at night.

Educators need to have a relationship with this voice, and need to work to seeing it in those they try to educate. If we want to make good decisions with people we are responsible for leading, if we want to make the meal a work of art, if we want to love the work we don't feel like doing, if we want to see our children in a new light, or we want to create something beautiful, then we need to be in touch with parts of ourselves that we only get inklings of, and to do that we need to let go and let our genius lead us.

TO BRING OUR WHOLE SELVES TO OUR ACTIVITY WE NEED TO BE IN PARTNERSHIP WITH OUR GENIUS.

One of the wonderful things about children under seven is that their several selves are still all one. One morning a kindergartner named Bianca, on her way into school, gave me a beautiful poster with many drawings and colors. She pointed out herself (the biggest figure) and the other students. She pointed out the school building, the sunshine, the trees, the flowers, and her mom (slightly smaller than herself). Letters across the sky spelled: "CHILDREN'S DAY SCHOOL." At the end of her narration, she pointed to the bottom of the picture and said, "These are the houses for the fairies," and then as a conspirator, she said, "I think there are fairies in the dirt."

I said, "Yes, Bianca, I am sure of it."

Bianca and I are not the only believers. There is, in fact, a fairy village in one corner of the playground where there is an abundance of sticks, stones, moss, dirt, and other building material. The kindergartners and first graders keep developing the fairy village year after year. Don't tell a seven-year-old there is no Santa Claus. Better for them to learn about the different kinds of reality later.

CEO or chef, gardener or educator, parent, poet or all of the above, we need to be enough of an authority to make good decisions. Whether we want to lead large groups of people or just lead our own lives, we all need to learn to lead and that means growing our authority.

Some authority is based on position, some authority is based on knowledge and expertise, some authority is granted by your people, but the only authority we can truly count on has its source in our genius. Alone in our prefrontal cortex we are at risk—not just for ourselves, but those around us. Listening to our genius is the only way to be liberated from our natural inclination to be arrogant.

Collective genius is the secret ingredient in all collaborations, all creative conflict and successful relationships. The only authority others can count on is authority that is informed by this genius, and followers of all ages—especially children—know when it is there and when it is not. To be an authority and open-minded at the same time—that's the trick our genius can help us with.

A mind that is unaware of its inner potential, a mind that is in denial of its secret longings, a mind that does not understand "Yes, Virginia, there is a Santa Claus," a mind that is not touched by myths, or out of touch with its dreams, or cannot see the fairies in the dirt, will not bring its whole self to the table and cannot thrive.

THE ORIGIN OF SELF-CONFIDENCE IS HAVING ENOUGH OF A RELATIONSHIP WITH YOUR UNKNOWN SELF THAT IT DOESN'T SCARE YOU INTO DENIAL.

This is why I get up before dawn and write, why I go for long walks, and why I listen to children. We are all divided selves, and trying to eliminate the inner schism is not a source of self-confidence but frustration. Making our broken selves whole is actually impossible. The origin of self-confidence is having enough of a relationship with your unknown self that it doesn't scare you into denial. Self-confidence is not a result of not having "issues," but of not letting the issues get in the way of taking responsibility.

As if it were yesterday, I recall several of us eighth graders standing around the desk of Mr. Burns, one of the best teachers I have ever known, asking him why he smoked. Mr. Burns said, "I'm nervous."

"Why are you nervous?" we asked.

"I am always nervous before class," he said.

Where does that strength come from? Can it be taught?

Yes. We can learn the disciplines of not letting our hidden self-compromise our self-confidence. For starters, we can practice vulnerability and experience the inner security we feel when we own the reality of our weaknesses. We can embrace our hidden self, give her a name and invite her into the classroom.

A thirty-year-old woman, an assistant professor, I once sat next to on a plane said, "I talk to my genius all day long."

"Really! That's wonderful," I said, then asked, "Why?"

"Remember, the relative not invited to the christening becomes the evil witch bent on our destruction."

Make friends with your genius.

Children want to be good decision-makers and are in search of adults who can lead. They need adults who can make decisions and take courageous stands. They need to see examples of people acting with courage, compassion and resilience. This search for integrity is why teenagers follow and idolize teachers with a strong center, people in touch with their genius. Their need is so great that they are contemptuous of adults who are out of touch with their genius. (It's not mature; it's not good; it's not graceful; but it is fair.)

To help children find their center, make good decisions, and grow their authority, it is important for children to see adults with authority, adults with a backbone, adults who will lead when leadership is called for. An authority vacuum is the opposite of a culture of arrogance, and the opposite of something bad is just as bad, if not worse.

Children don't need more words. They don't need a different curriculum. They don't need higher standards. They don't need a better test.

Children need practice in embracing conflict and making it creative. They need real-life social problem-solving—their own natural exercises in civility and kindness. They need to make mistakes and to learn from them. They need to be treated as whole people who are as passionate about building relationships as they are building their self-image.

The role of the adults is to coach them through these challenges, and for that we need adults who are, themselves, practiced in it. Of course, all people want to be somebody, somebody who has value in their world, somebody with integrity. Therefore, the central question for all educators, all the time is: Are *we* creating a culture where *we* get to be the way *we* want to be?

CHAPTER 30

In Times of Crisis the Nomenclature Must Be Changed

We think the breakdown comes because our life is in bad shape.
But maybe the ideas cause the disorder.

—James Hillman

As I said in the introduction, changing school culture entails changing our understanding and use of some key words. Here are my understandings of these words.

Character: We need to stop talking as if character is a set of virtues and understand character as the unique person we are in the act of becoming. The Greek *kharakter* means: the imprint that the gods put on your soul at birth.

Genius is the guiding spirit of a person, or place, or organization not a special intelligence. Genius is the voice of our soul calling us toward our character, our inner teacher, our calling. Our genius is the source of inspiration and enthusiasm, our muse. Genius is something each of us has rather than a few of us are.

Graceful: If a moment is graceful, it is because the players involved are in harmony with their genius. Our rational mind cannot know our whole self. Our rational mind is afraid of letting go. Letting go of control, judgment, mindset, outcomes, and self are essential for using imagination and creating graceful moments.

Leadership: It is not an elitist term. Leadership is defining yourself to the situation. Leadership is another name for self-actualization. Leadership is not something only a few of us have either by position or temperament. Leadership is something each of us is called to. We are called to leadership by our character. Rather than looking for "leadership qualities," we do better when we delight in characters in action. Being a leader and building your character are two names for the same thing.

Self is neither independent nor dependent but interdependent. Leadership is not a solitary business. If you feel "it's lonely at the top," you're not doing it right. We are our relationships.

Spirituality is bringing your whole self to a situation: mind, body, heart, and soul. Education and leadership are fundamentally spiritual activities. Religion is, of course, about spirituality, but spirituality is not necessarily about religion.

Authority: In an educational culture, authority is a good thing and exercised in such a way as to bring out the authority in others. All children are seen as decision makers and expected to want to contribute to their community. Learning how to tell the truth is an essential element of decision-making that grows authority, builds relationships, and brings out the best in all of us.

Intelligence: Intelligence is not something objectifiable on a test; intelligence is manifest in decisions. Cognitive skills, social skills, and emotional skills are intimately linked in all decisions. You can't have one without the other two, and you build it by making decisions.

Non-cognitive skills: The "Soft skills" and "non-cognitive skills" are hard, and they are highly cognitive. It's useful to think of them as disciplines like cleaning your brush before you paint with a different color.

Ability exists in action; it is not a static, objective, immutable commodity. Generalizing ability takes our eye off facing the challenge at hand with your whole self and making decisions. If an ability doesn't make a difference, does it exist? What if we simply stopped talking about ability altogether?

Diversity is about uniqueness of each of us, rather than a mixture of different kinds of people. When diversity is central to our culture, we transcend the generalizations we make about ourselves and others. A commitment to diversity is a commitment not to think of types of people. This concept of diversity is central to changing our minds about ability. There are not three kinds of people: gifted, normal, and those who "learn differently." Each brain is a unique combination of gifts and weaknesses and education is about helping each person maximize that brain in action. Diagnosing disabilities is dysfunctional.

Success is taking on challenges with enthusiasm.

Discipline is a good thing—an unqualified good thing. Disciplines are those behaviors, attitudes, and habits that help us accomplish our goals and become the characters we want to be.

Conflict: In most schools, where "conflict resolution" is taught, it is understood as a method for making conflict go away. In an educational culture, conflict is understood as a good thing, an opportunity to be creative, build your brain, grow your relationships, and build a better world. Good schools teach the disciplines of making conflict creative.

Courage is a discipline: a habit or a trait. Fearlessness is a characteristic of all learning cultures, because fear of failure, mistakes, diversity, loss, disappointment, and other challenges prevent learning.

Integrity is the whole thing not a "value." Integrity results from bringing our whole selves to a situation.

Enthusiasm is what integrity feels like. The Greek *enthousiasmos* means "imbued with the divine." The enthusiasm you feel when walked around a school and visit classes is the key metric for a great school that is truly delivering education. It's what makes teachers want to teach there, and parents want to send their children. Academic achievement follows enthusiasm. Enthusiasm is what we get when our collective genius is activated. Educators inspire (bring on the spirit), and so enthusiasm is our best metric.

Love is what enthusiasm feels like. Love is the end: children, teachers, and parents loving to go to school every day. Love is also the means. If I win and the other loses, I haven't won. Being "conflict averse" compromises our ability to love. By practicing the disciplines of turning conflict into collaboration, we engage our own genius and the genius of others, and the result is more truth, beauty, justice, grace, and love. Leading is learning how to love. Whether you are trying to make a relationship work or fix a broken school or anything in between, love is the beginning of our effort. Love is also the measure of our success. In between is a dance between leading and learning.

We have to understand that **education** is leading each character out into the world to contribute creatively and gracefully to it and that education is **leadership** and that leadership is education.

In the leadership moments in this book, we see that leadership is not an elitist term. Leadership is defining yourself to the situation—another name for self-actualization. Leadership is not something only a few of us have either by position or temperament. Leadership is something each of us is called to. We are called to leadership by our character. In these stories, we see characters in action, not "leadership qualities." We see that leadership is unique characters defining themselves to situations. In these moments, some inner voice, some muse, some genius, gave us our words, and showed how simple and powerful leadership can be when we focus on **collaborating**,

creating, and **contributing**. Being a leader and building your character are two names for the same thing.

As characters define themselves, they speak with **authority**. In fact, they express, define, and discover their authority simultaneously. The exercise of authority (an obvious goal of all education) entails **taking responsibility,** not just where our position makes it obvious that we should take responsibility, but for every situation we find ourselves in. Taking responsibility is a stance: I am responsible, not just for myself but also for my **relationships**, not fifty-fifty (because it "takes two to tango") but for the whole thing: all or nothing, regardless of what other people do.

Seeing this as the fundamental human challenge requires us to change our understanding of **intelligence**. Intelligence is not something objectifiable on a test; intelligence is manifest in decisions. Therefore, cognitive skills, social skills, and emotional skills are linked for all practical, real-life purposes. You can't have one without the other two. In fact, research with brain- damaged people reveal that, indeed, if any of these brain functions is compromised, a person's **decision-making** is compromised (Tony Damassio). There is no such thing as a "purely **rational**" decision. A prefrontal cortex divorced from its limbic system is severely compromised. If a person keeps making bad decisions, is it correct to call him intelligent?

In American culture **"Diversity"** is understood to be a matter of ethics, equity, and social justice. Diversity is understood as a moral good. And so it is in the fields of social, political, and economics. But in the interest of designing creative cultures (including but not limited to educational environments) diversity is more than a moral good; it is an essential. Diversity and the disciplines related to mobilizing diversity for the benefit of the group are some of the same disciplines required to bring out the best in others. The core concept of diversity work is that each person is unique; each person has a right and an obligation to define themselves and not be defined by the society they are in, and each person can make valuable contributions. Groups should not agree on a consensus until the quiet person has been asked.

Sometimes we want to know the intellectual diversity of a student body and are told what percent of the students **"gifted and talented,"** how many are **"normal,"** and how many **"learn differently."** What an obvious and disastrous distortion of reality. A class with twenty-five students has twenty-five different kinds of learners, and to maximize the potential of each student, they need to be taught as if they are. Once you have categorized kids, you have begun your trek down the wrong road. Worse: once a student has categorized herself, she has limited herself. Research shows that the **categories** in our heads are powerful predictors of our performance.

Categories are also powerful determiners of how we treat others. If we talk about "people with ADHD," for instance, our behaviors will derive from the understandings packed into this **mindset** rather than acting in the present, present to the unique human being in our presence. If we keep talking as if there are three kinds of people, teachers and parents will keep talking and acting as if it were true, even though it is obviously crazy.

People locked in ability-ist mindsets are in the sorting business, not the education business or the leadership business. In the education business, we love the unique **weirdness** of each person, love the marvelous diversity in each classroom and organize their work around the self-actualization of each individual. Furthermore, **followers** follow a lot better if they feel the person they are following cares about their unique character, their genius, their **soul**.

In creative cultures, people might say things like: "**Diversity is the solution, not the problem.**"

We have to stop talking about ability as if it were a static, objective, immutable commodity. Ability exists only in action.

IF A LEADER IS FEELING "IT'S LONELY AT THE TOP," HE IS PROBABLY NOT DOING HIS JOB PROPERLY

The leadership of great teachers gives us a peek into how a new notion of leadership can give us a new definition of what it means to be a **friend**. Being friendly comes naturally, but so does making enemies. This kind of **spiritual leadership** reveals a different kind of friendship—the kind where everyone is a friend. It doesn't have to be "lonely at the top" with this kind of friendship in mind (the sort of friendship embraced by Quakers, for instance). In fact, if a leader is lonely at the top, he is probably not doing his job properly and his leadership potential will be compromised, because **leadership happens in relationships.**

Educators are in the conflict business. Facing up to **conflict**, looking fear in the face, not being afraid of alienating others is where our power is. Maximizing **friendship** and minimizing enmity is the name of the human game, especially in the new world that is emerging before our very eyes. History will show that "terrorism," that monster that grabs our attention, is a rear-guard action of a retreating, obsolescent culture and world view. The real enemy is the human tendency to treat other humans as threats simply because they *could be* threats.

Living whole and happy lives requires leaning into **conflict**—embracing it, in fact. This requires learning the **disciplines** of making conflict creative, and some of these disciplines are counter-intuitive, and/or counter-cultural (Chapter 12, page 59). Leading a life requires that we keep practicing them. Harmonizing our needs, values, interests with the different needs, values and interests of others is the only way to go, and all these stories show that. If I win and the other loses, I haven't won. **Being "conflict averse" is not a virtue; it is another learning disability.** Practicing the disciplines of turning conflict into collaboration, we need to engage our own genius and the genius of others. **Truth, beauty, justice, love, and grace** are not possible without engaging this wisdom within us. And all this shows the how and the why of the reality that **love** is, actually, the answer.

Leaders in these stories face up to fear: we can imagine how we might apply this same trust in our genius to overcome all those other fears that compromise the leading of our lives: **failure, mistakes, diversity, loss, disappointment, and the other challenges** to which all lives are subjected. We can redefine what we mean by **success**, decide that mistakes are good, and understand how diversity is not a problem but a solution. Are we educators really trying to maximize learning? Then we have to embrace conflict, failure, mistakes, challenge, and diversity because, when you stop to think about it, this is where all the important learning takes place.

EDUCATION AND LEADERSHIP ARE FUNDAMENTALLY SPIRITUAL ACTIVITIES.

Education and **leadership** are fundamentally **spiritual** activities. To maximize "**results**," students and teachers, leaders, and followers must be **enthusiastic**. The Greek *enthousiasmos* means "imbued with the divine." To be successful teachers and leaders must **inspire** (bring on the spirit), and enthusiasm is our best metric. In four different cities in the course of thirty-six years, what made parents want their kids in my schools was the enthusiasm they saw when they visited classes and walked around the school. Almost no one ever asked about **test scores**. It was enthusiasm that made teachers want to teach there. Academic **achievement** follows enthusiasm, and everyone actually seems to know that. Enthusiasm is what you get when our collective genius is activated.

If a moment is **graceful**, it is because the players involved are in harmony with their genius. Our **rational mind** cannot know our whole **self**. Our rational mind even knows it doesn't know but is afraid of letting go. Letting go of **control, judgment, mindset, outcomes,** and **self** are essential for using imagination, creating something new, and creating graceful moments. **Integrity** is not a "value," it's the whole thing. Integrity is what it feels like when we bring our whole selves to a situation.

When leaders are successful, the people experience what one might call a **collective genius.** Carl Jung was right. There is a collective unconscious.

The unconscious it not evil. It has a voice. And remember: the relative that didn't get invited to the christening became the evil witch.

The core concept embedded in our new glossary of terms is that a **leader's job** is to define her **character** in such a way as to increase the **authority** of others, thus creating a **relationships** in which all people define their unique characters in partnership with their **genius**. These concepts are central to a **loving, learning, leadership culture.**

"Education is **leadership**; management kills learning," "Arrogance, **conflict aversion, perfectionism** and staying positive are all learning disabilities," "**Challenges** are opportunities," and "**Education** is leading each person's genius out into the world to contribute creatively, effectively, and gracefully to it." These are some of the concepts that need to be sloganized.

Conclusion

Education is the drawing out of the soul

—Ralph Waldo Emerson

Maggie Doyne awoke one morning at the age of eighteen with the profound fear that after thirteen years of school "I knew very little about myself and what I wanted in my life." She said that school taught her "some kinds of knowledge but nothing of the inside sort of things." She decided to postpone college and get herself out into the world. In the course of the next five years, she discovered other worlds and peoples, depths of human suffering and joy she didn't know existed, and in the course of the next five years, she built an orphanage and a school for two hundred children and "got my passion back to live and to learn and to be human on this earth."

She says, "I was lucky that I woke up with that when I was eighteen."

Maggie's story is not so much about Maggie doing good but about Maggie engaging her genius in the education of her character. For this is our core business; that is, to lead each character out into the world to function creatively, effectively, and gracefully within it.

Is Maggie well educated? What does that mean?

If she is, who can take credit for it? Her parents? Her school?

Is she just lucky for her genes, her home life, her socio-economic place in society?

What does this say about what metrics we should use to evaluate the quality of education?

I'm sure Maggie's parents are proud of her, but are they proud of the outcome, her career, that she is making a difference, or are they proud of how she is going about it, how she is leading her life?

Happiness, success, winning, and achievement are not what we should wish for our children but rather the grit to live in life's tensions—the confidence to learn from conflict, mistakes, disappointment, failure, loneliness, and losing. When a person is fully herself, she is also harmonizing herself with her environment. The fulfillment of Maggie includes her constructive impact on the environment. This is the essence of integrity—wholeness that includes what is good for self as well as others.

Who is driving what goes on in schools, and toward what interests? Are educational reforms intended to regain our competitive edge in the world? To keep our jobs from going to foreigners? to serve the needs of corporate America? Should we evaluate schools on the basis of test scores? How many graduates go to college? What their occupations are after college?

These questions seem important as we consider a course for American education. The debates, however, are ancillary to the core purpose of education: bringing out the best in each child in our care.

What should a school be? A school should be an education, of course, but what is that? Education is leading each unique character out into the world to contribute creatively, collaboratively, and gracefully to it.

To deliver on this mission, a school must bring people together to create a culture, a culture that educates, a culture that teaches the disciplines of leading, thinking critically, creating, and collaborating.

To be an education, a school must focus on students as agents rather than recipients. In such a school, teachers aren't held accountable for doing things to students and recording the results. They are not held accountable for covering a curriculum, but rather for using the curriculum as a vehicle for students to build their brains and become the unique characters their genius is leading them to become. Teachers are held accountable for creating the conditions for optimal learning by focusing students' energy on collaborating, creating, and being valuable.

Creating something new that is valuable requires understanding how things are, how things work, how they relate and understanding all these dimensions well enough to come up with a hypothesis about something new that would make a difference. An educational culture builds the confidence to test these hypotheses with increasing frequency and complexity. Everyone comes out of such a school knowing they can make a difference because in thirteen years of school they have had 2,340 days of experience making a difference.

Therefore, a school must be a place for having wonderful ideas, trying them out, changing our minds, creating value, disagreeing creatively, arguing lovingly, and resolving disputes justly. Solving a social problem requires at least as much brainpower as a typical algebra problem and both should be taught as creative endeavors. Those "soft, non-cognitive skills" that are the secret of success are highly cognitive, hard, and best learned in real-life, socially rich challenges.

"She believed in me" is so often the report of a young person whose life went from despair to success. Simply saying, "I believe in you," however, never really does the trick. Challenging someone to show what they can do and being with them as they show you is what believe-in-you looks like. This is the essence of education, and it must be embedded in the culture of every school.

Today, humanity is working on the nearly incomprehensible project of building one world community. When we watch enormous containerships come and go, when we maneuver through airports and big cities or open our digital devices, we see it happening before our very eyes. In the process, cultures are changing, and the tribalism, racism, sectarianism, that often characterize a culture are becoming more obviously obsolete.

Creating, collaborating, and contributing are increasingly obvious as required skillsets for human success. The need to create is qualifying the pressure to be right. The call to collaborate is moderating solo virtuosity. The imperative to contribute is preempting "look out for yourself." Self-made, arrogant men are becoming increasingly unpopular as the solitary, autocratic, directive leader becomes more obviously dysfunctional. The apparent popularity of Donald Trump in the last decade, for instance, is the rear-guard phenomenon of an obsolescent culture.

However, some cultures—especially school cultures—are not changing fast enough to prepare people for the world that is becoming. Millions of Americans are being brought up in antique cultures and left in the dust. We need to focus our creativity on creating cultures that foster creativity, collaboration, and being valuable to others.

For the last hundred and fifty years, Americans have observed the failure of schools to educate. Leaders like Francis Parker, Susan Blow, John Dewey, Clara Baker, Elizabeth Irwin, Maria Montessori, and many others designed new delivery systems based on the uniqueness of each child, their needs to self-direct and self-actualize, and their need to be socially competent and emotionally strong. There are thousands of such schools all over the world. We need millions.

Schools like these are consistently marginalized by the label "alternative education." They are, actually, delivering *real* education. Even though they consistently turn out strong, academically prepared young people who are on the path to success, they are often labeled as "soft" on "the basics" and "academic excellence."

Research in the last thirty years has convinced most people that the social-emotional skills are even more predictive of success than measures of academic achievement or "cognitive skills," and this has motivated more pressure to revolutionize education. But schools are famous for suffering new initiatives without improving.

If social-emotional skills are taught in the old model, it will not make the difference we want it to make. The students will learn their SES from the social context. Are disagreements, conflicts, and diversity embraced and understood as great learning opportunities? Imagine a school where "Builds on other people's ideas," "Knows when to lead and when to follow," "Listens with a willingness to change," "Uses mistakes as learning opportunities," are metrics. Even if all we cared about were the three R's, we must teach them in the context of a culture high in the three C's: Collaborating, Creating, and Contributing.

The medical profession has a hypocritic oath. The education profession needs a Socratic Oath. Here's my proposal for one:

> *I will watch for, believe in, notice, love and engage the genius of those in my charge.*

If this were our Socratic Oath, we would send young people into the world who (a) keep America competitive, (b) help to strengthen the local community and the global economy, (c) supply good workers for the work force, (d) further the cause of democracy, (e) maximize students' chances of getting into the next appropriate level of academia, and (f) are highly practiced at creating, loving, thriving, and making a difference in the world .

My dream is that all parents, teachers, and all those responsible for children would take the Socratic Oath, that they would let nothing (not standardized tests, curricula, school district policies and procedures, the anxiety of other adults, their own fear of failure, etc.) . . . nothing get in the way of holding true to that oath, and that no child in the world were without an adult who has taken the oath on their behalf.

The end of education is self-actualization, but self-actualization is intimately related to our skills at actualizing harmony and partnership with others who are pursuing their own self-actualization. So, we need to build on our natural need to collaborate and contribute. At home, at school and in the work place our focus should be to optimize our need to be valuable to others and to make a difference in the world. Children are ready for this. They want it. They are wired for it. And for this, everyone in the organization needs to be on a mission greater than ourselves. Children instinctively know this. Why don't we?

APPENDIX

Counter-Cultural Habits, Mores and Myths

Essential Skills in Learning Organizations

1. Treat people as if they know what they are doing.
2. If you want to get them thinking, ask them what *they* think. Listen with a willingness to change.
3. Talk to kids the same way you talk to adults.
4. Go directly to the person you have a problem with.
5. Go directly to the person who can do something about it.
6. Be kind. Always start there.
7. Be accurate not "positive" or "negative"—find the right words.
8. Use descriptive language and insist on it in others. Don't label. Speak so that it plays like a movie in our heads. Deliver feedback that is hearable, seeable, and doable.
9. Get good at talking about hard things.
10. Remove the recrimination layer.
11. Treat people the way you would most fondly hope they would be rather than the person you are afraid they are (or rather than the _____ they are proving themselves to be.)
12. Be prepared with your best move if it turns out you *are* actually not dealing with a potential friend.
13. Treat people the way *they* want to be treated. (The golden rule is flawed.)
14. Begin a sentence with "My integrity requires . . ." (The bedrock of your authority is your integrity.)
15. Take responsibility (all or nothing; not fifty-fifty).
16. Play your position.

17. Don't get mad; get creative.
18. See all challenges as opportunities.
19. Do the present right and the future will take care of yourself.
20. Change your mind.

Mores of Learning Communities

1. To maximize achievement, focus on learning rather than achievement.
2. "Learning differences" is not a euphemism; we all have them.
3. Good teachers teach as if we all learn differently.
4. Education is exercises in imperfection. Truth and beauty are achieved through a process of collective successive approximation.
5. Useful creativity springs from relationships.
6. The measure of our authority is the degree to which we increase *their* authority.
7. "Discipline is a good thing—an unqualified good thing. Disciplines are those skills, habits, and attitudes that help us accomplish our goals."
8. Changing your mind is a good thing.
9. The quality of a community is a function of the things we can't talk about (an inverse function).
10. People have difficult conversations.
11. Tell the truth in a common language: describe, describe, describe. Speak so it plays like a movie in their heads. Stories are data.
12. Arrogance, conflict avoidance, perfection, and defensiveness are learning disabilities.
13. Mistakes, failure, criticism, difference, and conflict are welcomed as opportunities to learn.
14. Good leadership brings out leadership in others.
15. If it is not fun or meaningful, it is not sustainable.
16. All problems are personnel problems and you are "personnel."
17. At the core of these problems is the question: "Who am I in the world?"
18. Success is failing again and again without losing enthusiasm (NOT "The higher up the socio-economic pyramid you get the more successful and happier you will be.")
19. Success looks like: taking responsibility (all or nothing; not fifty-fifty).
20. Success is continuous development of your decision-making mechanism.
21. People welcome challenge. (NOT Challenges are bad. "He is challenged" is a euphemism for disabled.)
22. Make as many mistakes as you can as early as you can. (NOT: Avoid mistakes).
23. Conflict Is Our Business; Get Good at It (NOT Conflict is bad).
24. Leaders turn conflicts into collaborations.

New Myths for Educational Cultures

1. Self-actualization is self-creation through endless interaction. (NOT simply "being yourself." Being yourself is the challenge of each moment, and self changes in the interaction.)
2. Self-actualization is the name of the game for all ages (NOT the end game available to only 1–2 percent of the population.)
3. Self-actualization is another name for leadership (defining yourself to the situation.)
4. Self-actualization is being in love all the time.
5. Performance is a function of struggle (NOT intelligence).
6. Intelligence is something we grow as we take on challenges (NOT something we are born with.)
7. Children are born with empathy. (NOT "We have to teach kids empathy.")
8. Children are internally motivated to master the challenges of social responsibility. (NOT: "Children are born selfish.")
9. Children naturally want to make a difference. (NOT: We have to instill a sense of service in them.)
10. All kindergarteners come to school to try to make something of themselves.
11. Kids are in the process of discovering their gifts, and none of them are normal.
12. They each learn differently, and they know it. (NOT: Three kinds of people: "Gifted and Talented, Average, and those who have Learning Differences.")
13. The "soft" and "non-cognitive" skills are hard, cognitive, and essential.
14. Cognitive, emotional, and social abilities are inseparable.
15. Decision making requires cognitive *and* emotional *and* social intelligence. (NOT: "Emotions interfere with good decision making.")
16. Humans are naturally good at conflict (Our branch of the primate line got good at it to survive.)
17. Take responsibility (all or nothing; NOT fifty-fifty. NOT: "It takes two to tango.")
18. Diversity is the solution; not the problem (NOT: a matter of ethics, or morality or at odds with academic achievement but essential for excellent education.)
19. Each of us has a genius. (NOT: A few of us are geniuses.)
20. Our genius cares passionately about others and relationships. (NOT: Selfish).
21. Our geniuses are in league with each other (NOT: "Look out for Number 1.").

Our geniuses are in league with each other. (NOT: "Look out for Number One.")

Notes

Chapter 5

1. Carol Dweck, *Mindset: The New Psychology of Success* (Ballentine Books, N.Y., 2007).
2. Tony Wagner, *Seven Survival Skills* in *The Global Achievement Gap* (Basic Books, 2010).
3. Ellen Galinsky, *Mind in the Making* (Harper Collins, 2010).

Chapter 8

1. Alison Gopnik, *The Scientist in the Crib: What Early Learning Tells Us about the Mind* (Mariner Books, 1999).

Chapter 9

1. Martin Haberman, "The Pedagogy of Poverty Versus Good Teaching" (*Phi Delta Kappan*, December 1999).

Chapter 11

1. Kathryn Shultz, *Being Wrong* (HarperCollins, 2010).
2. Argyris C., and Schon, D.A. (1978) *Organizational Learning: A theory of action perspective*. Reading, MA: Addison Wesley.

Chapter 12

1. Roger Fisher, *Getting to Yes* (Penguin Books, 2011).

Chapter 14

1. Rudolf Steiner, *Kingdom of Childhood* (Rudolf Steiner Press, 1982).
2. Tomorrow's Change Makers: Reclaiming the Power of Citizenship for a New Generation, Marilyn Price-Mitchell, PhD | Sep 16, 2015.
3. To be taught empathy as thoughtfulness (Winn and Bloom https://www.youtube.com/watch?v=FRvVFW85IcU2013).

Chapter 15

1. Ralph Waldo Emerson, "*Self-Reliance*" (1841). (Emersoncentral.com).
2. https://www.youtube.com/watch?v=NS2PqTTxFFc.
3. https://www.youtube.com/watch?v=9DuW5gGN0_0.

Chapter 16

1. David Brooks, "Social Animal" (*The New Yorker*, January 17, 2011).

Chapter 22

1. https://www.simplypsychology.org/Erik-Erikson.html.
2. https://www.simplypsychology.org/maslow.html.

Chapter 27

1. Carol Dweck, https://www.mindsetworks.com/Science/Default.

Chapter 28

1. Alison Gopnik, Partricia Kuhl, *The Scientist in the Crib: What Early Learning Tells Us about the Mind* (New York, 2010).

Author Biography

Rick Ackerly is a nationally recognized educator and speaker with forty-five years of experience working in and for schools. With a Master's in Education from Harvard, he served as head of five schools and, today, speaks to parent and school groups across the country. He is the author of *The Genius in Every Child: Encouraging Character, Curiosity and Creativity in Children*, 2012. His blog is www.geniusinchildren.org.

www.ingramcontent.com/pod-product-compliance
Lightning Source LLC
Chambersburg PA
CBHW032025230426
43671CB00005B/209